Collected Poems for Children

Gareth Owen was born and raised in Ainsdale, Lancashire, where his main ambition was to play inside forward for Everton and England. He left school at sixteen for the merchant navy but was invalided out after falling from a mast in Buenos Aires.

After various jobs (factory work, bookselling, clerical work) he attended Bretton Hall Training College as a mature student and taught Drama and English in a Secondary Modern School in Ilford before becoming a lecturer at Bordesley College, Birmingham.

There he began to write poems, novels, plays and musicals and also did some acting and directing. He formed a fringe theatre company and for a time he managed the career of soul singer Ruby Turner and ran his own record company.

He reads his work regularly in schools but also enjoys reciting the work of other writers in colleges and arts festivals up and down the country. He reads regularly for the BBC and for two years presented Radio 4's long-running *Poetry Please*.

He now lives in Ludlow, Shropshire.

Gareth Owen

Collected Poems
for Children

MACMILLAN
CHILDREN'S BOOKS

First published 2000 by Macmillan Children's Books
a division of Macmillan Publishers Limited
25 Eccleston Place, London SW1W 9NF
Basingstoke and Oxford
www.macmillan.co.uk

Associated companies throughout the world

ISBN 0 333 78078 7

1 3 5 7 9 8 6 4 2

A CIP catalogue record for this book is available from
the British Library.

Phototypeset by Intype London Ltd
Printed and bound in Great Britain by
Mackays of Chatham plc, Kent

For Alice, Lily, Linda and Natascha

Contents

SONG OF THE CITY

MY GRANNY IS A SUMO WRESTLER

Salford Road

Cycling down the street
to meet my friend John

On my bike and down our street,
Swinging round the bend,
Whizzing past the Library,
Going to meet my friend.

Silver flash of spinning spokes,
Whirr of oily chain,
Bump of tyre on railway line
Just before the train.

The road bends sharp at Pinfold Lane
Like a broken arm,
Brush the branches of the trees
Skirting Batty's Farm.

Tread and gasp and strain and bend
Climbing Gallows' Slope,
Flying down the other side
Like an antelope.

Swanking into Johnnie's street,
Cycling hands on hips,
Past O'Connors corner shop
That always smells of chips.

Bump the door of his backyard
Where we always play,
Lean my bike and knock the door,
'Can John come out to play?'

Going to the Dentist

After tea
Trev and me
Have to go up to Whinnick
And visit the clinic
To have our teeth looked at. My mum makes me go every
month. I think that's overdoing things but there's no
arguing with her.

We sit down
Look around
There are three in the queue
We both say, 'After you',
At exactly the same moment but in the end I know it's going
to be me that goes in first. Always is. Still, there's
something to be said for getting it over with.

I spend an age
Reading the Sporting Page
Trev shuffles on his seat
And swings his nervous feet
about all over the place trying to look right casual but I
know all the time that inside he's as scared as I am.

An old man blows
His old man's nose;
Clock strikes six.
Bite nails, count the ticks
But time doesn't half drag. Perhaps we're too late. Perhaps
he won't have time to see us. After I've counted a hundred
he'll come out looking sad and tell us to go home. But he
doesn't.

A baby cries
A mother sighs
And lifts her on her knee.
Wonder what he'll do to me?
Please don't let him take any out. Or give me gas. I can't
stand gas. Anything but gas. Anything that is except the
needle. Or the drill. Anything except the drill. I want to go
home.

Or a filling
Can be killing.
Cough, look without a care
But inside I say a prayer
Promising to clean my teeth three times a day and four times
on Sunday until the day I die as long as he doesn't do any
fillings or take any out and there's no gas or injections.
Another thing about this dentist they say he used to be an
SS officer but I'm not sure if there's much truth in that.

Only Trev and me
For the dentist to see.
I wonder, staring at the wall,
Why we have any teeth at all;
I'm sure we could get along without them. I wouldn't mind
living on milk and mashed potato or even sucking
everything through a straw.

The dentist looks at me.
'Open wide, let me see.'
Tongue's huge, throat dry
But I heave a sigh
of relief when he says my teeth are all right and I don't have
to come back for another three months. Funny how I forget
all the promises I've made.

Trev tries to grin
As he goes in.
'What's he like? Did he take any out? What did he do?'
'Oh, he filled a few, took out one or two, there's nothing to
it at all.'
And I clap him on the back as he goes past. He looks very
white suddenly. I put my hands in my pockets and look out
of the window. Traffic rumbles by. Sun shines. Wonder what
we'll have for supper?

My Dog Robbo

Mongrel dog Robbo up got,
Thumped 'is ol' tail
What's tied up loose like an undone granny
And wagger-wagged it quite a lot.

Mongrel body on four sticks,
Mongrel napper full of tricks,
Mongrel pelt stuffed with ticks,
Mongrel gob wet of licks.

Scraps out, sups all,
Nabs all eyes light on,
Scoffs tin tacks and half bricks,
Chews all teeth bite on.

Knocks the purr out of pussies,
Fights the legs on our bed,
Woofs the wind up red buses
And leaves them for dead.

Howl like a squeaky brake,
Stink like a bog,
You get under the world's skin
That's Robbo my dog.

Salford Road

Salford Road, Salford Road,
Is the place where I was born,
With a green front gate, a red brick wall
And hydrangeas round a lawn.

Salford Road, Salford Road,
Is the road where we would play
Where the sky lay over the roof tops
Like a friend who'd come to stay.

The Gardeners lived at fifty-five,
The Lunds with the willow tree,
Mr Pool with the flag and the garden pond
And the Harndens at fifty-three.

There was riding bikes and laughing
Till we couldn't laugh any more,
And bilberries picked on the hillside
And picnics on the shore.

I lay in bed when I was four
As the sunlight turned to grey
And heard the train through my pillow
And the seagulls far away.

And I rose to look out of my window
For I knew that someone was there
And a man stood as sad as nevermore
And didn't see me there.

And when I stand in Salford Road
And think of the boy who was me
I feel that from one of the windows
Someone is looking at me.

My friends walked out one Summer day,
Walked singing down the lane,
My friends walked into a wood called Time
And never came out again.

We live in a land called Gone-Today
That's made of bricks and straw
But Salford Road runs through my head
To a land called Evermore.

Sports Report

Five o'clock of a Saturday night,
November out of doors,
We sit down to tea,
My family and me,
To hear the football scores.

I'm the one in our family who tries to listen but everyone
else just talks and talks and talks.

Dad discusses his rose trees,
Stephen chokes on his bread,
Grandad moans
About the cold in his bones
And talks about people who're dead.

Betty dreams about Terry,
'Who's handsome and ever so tall.'
When Mum joins in
There's such a din
You can't hear the scores at all.

Well a few, but the worst is only hearing half a result, that's
very frustrating that is.

Did Fulham win at Fratton Park?
Did Millwall lose at the Den?
What happened to Blackpool at Boothferry Park?
Did Doncaster draw again?

Who dropped a point at Derby?
A fight in the crowd at where?
'There's a terrible draught,
I'm freezing to death
And nobody seems to care.'

Who was sent off at Southampton?
Who was booked at West Ham?
'I'm pleased with that rose.'
'Stop picking your nose.'
'Will somebody pass me the jam.'

The Owls beat the Blades in a derby,
Cardiff beat Carlisle three-nil.
'He looks ever so young
With his hair all long.'
'Will someone fetch Grandad his pill.'

Someone lost at the Valley,
The Orient somehow got four.
'You're not to eat jam
With your fingers young man,
You get the knife from the drawer.'

Plymouth Argyle whipped Walsall,
Darlington managed a draw.
'Our Betty, stop dreamin'
And look after Stephen,
He's pouring the sauce on the floor.'

Wrexham romped home at The Racecourse,
The Sandgrounders' winger got three.
'With a touch of compost
And some luck with the frost
We might get some blooms on that tree.'

I've missed Albion and City and Chelsea,
Queens Park and Chester and Crewe.
'Get your grandad his scarf,
There's no need to laugh
We don't want him dying of flu.'

A sudden reversal at Reading,
A last minute winner at York.
'Turn down that radio!
D'you hear what I say to you
I can hardly hear myself talk.'

Yes, but you wait till she wants to listen to something,
I'm not even allowed to breathe. Just to be awkward
everybody goes quiet when the Scottish results come on.

Those strange-sounding teams up in Scotland,
Kilmarnock and Brechin and Clyde,
And players with names like Macintosh,
MacDonald, McNab and MacBride.

Who wants to know about Berwick
Or Forfar, Stranraer and Dundee,
That Hibernian were humbled at Hampden,
That Stirling slammed Celtic eight-three?

The only thing left to do is to go and get the paper.
Trouble is I haven't any money left.

Mum starts clearing the table,
Stacking the plates in the sink.
Would Dad think it funny
If I borrowed some money
To buy the *Sporting Pink?*

While Mum's out of the room he slips me five pence.
I'll have to pay him back of course. He's very strict about
things like that, my dad.

I race through the fog up to Jackson's,
Pumping out breath like steam.
I've got to find out
How United made out
They're my favourite team.

So I run my finger down the list of scores looking for the
result.

United, United, United.
Never mind about the rest.
They've won, they've won,
Like they ought to have done,
Through a last minute header from Best.

When your team wins everything's all right.

I shuffle through leaves in the gutter,
Whistle a tune through my teeth,
Tightrope on walls,
Head imaginary balls,
My family's not bad underneath.

Winter

On Winter mornings in the playground
The boys stand huddled,
Their cold hands doubled
Into trouser pockets.
The air hangs frozen
About the buildings
And the cold is an ache in the blood
And a pain on the tender skin
Beneath fingernails.
The odd shouts
Sound off like struck iron
And the sun
Balances white
Above the boundary wall.
I fumble my bus ticket
Between numb fingers
Into a fag,
Take a drag
And blow white smoke
Into the December air.

Our School

I go to Weld Park Primary,
It's near the Underpass
And five blocks past the Cemetery
And two roads past the Gas
Works with the big tower that smells so bad
  me and me mates put our hankies over our
    faces and pretend we're being attacked
      by poison gas . . . and that.

There's this playground with lines for rounders,
And cricket stumps chalked on the wall,
And kids with their coats for goalposts
Booting a tennis ball
Around all over the place and shoutin' and arguin'
  about offside and they always kick it over
    the garden wall next door and she
      goes potty and tells our head teacher
        and he gets right ratty with
          everybody and stops us playin'
            football . . .
              . . . and everything.

We have this rule at our school
You've to wait till the whistle blows
And you can't go in till you hear it
Not even if it snows.

And your wellies get filled with water and your socks
go all soggy and start slipping down your legs
and your hands get so cold they go all
crumpled and you can't undo
the buttons of your mac when
you do get inside . . .
. . . it's true.

The best thing is our classroom.
When it's fine you can see right far,
Past the Catholic Cathedral
Right to the Morris Car
Works where me dad works as a fitter and sets off
right early every morning in these overalls
with his snap in this sandwich box and
a flask of tea and always moanin'
about the money . . . honest.

In Hall we pray for brotherly love
And sing hymns that are ever so long
And the Head shouts at Linda Nutter
Who's always doing wrong.
She can't keep out of trouble because
she's always talkin'
she can't stop our teacher says she
must have been injected with
a gramophone needle she talks
so much and
that made me laugh once
not any more though I've heard it
too often . . . teachers!

Loving your enemy sounds all right
Until you open your eyes
And you're standing next to Nolan
Who's always telling lies
About me and getting me into trouble and about
  three times a week I fight him after school
    it's like a habit I've got
      but I can't love him even though
        I screw my eyes up real hard and try like
          mad, but if it wasn't him it
            would be somebody else
              I mean
                you've got to have enemies . . .
                  . . . haven't you?

We sing 'O to be a pilgrim'
And think about God and heaven
And then we're told the football team lost
By thirteen goals to seven
But that's not bad because St Xavier's don't half have
  big lads in their team and last time we played
    they beat us eighteen one and this time
      we got seven goals . . .
        . . . didn't we?

Then we have our lessons,
We have Science and English and Maths,
Except on Wednesday morning
When our class goes to the baths
And it's not half cold and Peter Bradberry's
  fingers went all wrinkled and blue last week
    and I said, 'You're goin' to die, man'
      but he pushed me under the water and I had to
       hold my breath for fifteen minutes.
        But he's still alive though . . .
         . . . he is.

Friday's my favourite day though,
We have Art all afternoon
And I never care what happens
Cos I know it's home-time soon
And I'm free for two whole days but I think
  sometimes it wouldn't be half so good
    having this weekend if we didn't have five
      days
        of
          school
            in
              between—
Would it?

Sharon's Life

My name is Sharon
I have two brothers
Called Phillip and William
Sometimes they bother me
But often they don't.
Being me is fun.
When it is older
It won't be so good I think.
Phillip lost my book
It had pictures
He lost it
But I am not very cross.
Daddy bought it.
Aunt Judy died last week
Mummy said it was a loss
And then she cried
Quite a bit.
My dog is called Spot
He has some bad habits.
Perhaps I will find the book.
My bed is green.
I'm five.
That's all.
I'm glad I'm alive.

The Cat

When the moon is leering yellow
And the trees are witches' claws
That scratch upon the window panes
And scrape upon the doors,
I crouch before the fireplace
And smirk into the heat
And think of wild adventures
That are waiting up the street –
But I'm tooooo tiiiiired.

I could slink along the alleyway
That's sentinelled with bins
And nose inside old papers
And lick the empty tins.
I could sniff out mice in the Railway Yard
Or watch the Midnight Mail
Thunder through the station
Rattling his angry tail –
But I'm tooooo laaaaazy.

I could tease the dogs in the school-yard
Pretending they're not there
And swagger in front of their noses
With my head up in the air
And when they start to chase me
And howl and tumble and call
I'd nimbly leap from their snapping jaws
And smile at them from the wall –
But I'm tooooo sleeeeepy.

I could go and meet the tabby
Who only comes out at night
And the rather belligerent ginger
Who lost his ear in a fight.
I'll howl, I'll miaowl by the lamp post,
I'll race, I'll roister, I'll roam,
I'll wander the night by the moon's yellow light
I'll never want to go home . . .
Tomooooorooooow.

Saturdays

Real
Genuine
Saturdays
Like marbles
Conkers
Sweet new potatoes
Have their especial season;
Are all morning
With midday at five o'clock.
True Saturdays
Are borrowed from early Winter
And the left overs
Of Autumn sunshine days
But separate from days of snow.
The skies dine on dwindles of smoke
Where leafy plots smoulder
With small fires.
Sunday meat is bought
And late
Large, white loaves
From little corner shops.
People passing
Wave over garden walls,
Greengrocers and milkmen are smiled upon
And duly paid.
It is time for the chequered tablecloth
And bowls of soup.
And early on
We set out with some purpose
Through only

Lovely Saturday,
Under skies
Like sun-shot water,
For the leccy train
And the Match in Liverpool.

Denis Law

I live at 14 Stanhope Street,
Me mum, me dad and me,
And three of us have made a gang,
John Stokes and Trev and me.

Our favourite day is Saturday;
We go Old Trafford way
And wear red colours in our coats
To watch United play.

We always stand behind the goal
In the middle of the roar.
The others come to see the game –
I come for Denis Law.

His red sleeves flap around his wrists,
He's built all thin and raw,
But the toughest backs don't stand a chance
When the ball's near Denis Law.

He's a whiplash when he's in control,
He can swivel like an eel,
And twist and sprint in such a way
It makes defences reel.

And when he's hurtling for the goal
I know he's got to score.
Defences may stop normal men –
They can't stop Denis Law.

We all race home when full time blows
To kick a tennis ball,
And Trafford Park is our back-yard,
And the stand is next door's wall.

Old Stokesey shouts, 'I'm Jimmy Greaves,'
And scores against the door,
And Trev shouts: 'I'll be Charlton,' –
But I am Denis Law.

Boredom

Boredom
Is
Me
Gloomy as Monday
Moidering the time away
Murdering the holiday
Just
Sort of waiting.

Boredom
Is
Clouds
Black as old slate
Chucking rain straight
On our Housing Estate
All grey
Day long.

Boredom
Is
John
In bed again
The trickle of rain
On the window pane
And no one
To play with.

Boredom
Is
Trev
Gone for the day
To Colwyn Bay
For a holiday
And me
On my own.

Boredom
Is
My comics all read
The Library closed
Damp clothes before the fire
Deciding
Not to clean my bike
To tidy my room
To help with the washing up.

Boredom
Is
Empty streets
And black telegraph poles
A muddy tractor
On the building site
Shipwrecked in mud.

Boredom
Is
A thick circle
Of emptiness
Heaviness
Nothingness
With me
Slumped in the middle.

Boredom
Is
Boredom
Boredom is
Boredom
Is
Boredom
Boredom is
Boredom
Is
Boredom
Boredom is
Boredom
Is
Boredom
Boredom is
Boredom
Is
Boredom
Boredom is
Boredom
Is
Boredom
Boredom is
Boredom
Is
Boredom
Boredom is

Jonah and the Whale

Well, to start with
It was dark
So dark
You couldn't see
Your hand in front of your face;
And huge
Huge as an acre of farmland.
How do I know?
Well, I paced it out
Length and breadth
That's how.
And if you was to shout
You'd hear your own voice resound,
Bouncing along the ridges of its stomach,
Like when you call out
Under a bridge
Or in an empty hall.
Hear anything?
No not much,
Only the normal
Kind of sounds
You'd expect to hear
Inside a whale's stomach;
The sea swishing far away,
Food gurgling, the wind
And suchlike sounds;
Then there was me screaming for help,
But who'd be likely to hear,
Us being miles from
Any shipping lines

And anyway
Supposing someone did hear,
Who'd think of looking inside a whale?
That's not the sort of thing
That people do.
Smell? I'll say there was a smell.
And cold. The wind blew in
Something terrible from the South
Each time he opened his mouth
Or took a swallow of some tit bit.
The only way I found
To keep alive at all
Was to wrap my arms
Tight around myself
And race from wall to wall.
Damp? You can say that again;
When the ocean came sluicing in
I had to climb his ribs
To save myself from drowning.
Fibs? You think I'm telling you fibs,
I haven't told the half of it brother.
I'm only giving a modest account
Of what these two eyes have seen
And that's the truth on it.
Here, one thing I'll say
Before I'm done –
Catch me eating fish
From now on.

This and That

Two cats together
In bee-heavy weather
After the August day
In smug contentment lay
By the garden shed
In the flower bed
Yawning out the hours
In the shade of the flowers
And they passed the time away,
Between stretching and washing and sleeping,
Talking over the day.

'Climbed a tree.'
'Aaaah.'
'Terrorized sparrows.'
'Mmmmh.'
'Was chased.'
'Aaaah.'
'Fawned somewhat!'
'Mmmmh.'
'Washed, this and that,'
Said the first cat.

And they passed the time away
Between stretching and washing and sleeping
Talking over the day.

'Gazed out of parlour window.'
'Aaaah.'
'Pursued bluebottles.'
'Mmmmh.'
'Clawed curtains.'
'Aaaah.'
'Was cuffed.'
'Mmmmh.'
'Washed, this and that,'
Said the other cat.

And they passed the time away
Between stretching and washing and sleeping
Talking over the day.

'Scratched to be let in.'
'Aaaah.'
'Patrolled the house.'
'Mmmmh.'
'Scratched to go out.'
'Aaaah.'
'Was booted.'
'Mmmmh.'
'Washed, this and that,'
Said the first cat.

And they passed the time away
Between stretching and washing and sleeping
Talking over the day.

'Lapped cream elegantly.'
'Aaaah.'
'Disdained din-din.'
'Mmmmh.'
'Borrowed a little salmon.'
'Aaaah.'
'Was tormented.'
'Mmmmh.'
'Washed, this and that,'
Said the other cat.

And they passed the time away
Between stretching and washing and sleeping
Talking over the day.

'Chased a shadow or two.'
'Aaaah.'
'Met friends.'
'Mmmmh.'
'Sang a little.'
'Aaaah.'
'Avoided water.'
'Mmmmh.'
'Washed, this and that,'
Said the first cat.

And they passed the time away
Between stretching and washing and sleeping
Talking over the day.

Photograph

Is that you and is that me
Captured by photography?
Is that Auntie, is that Dad?
Is that face the face I had?

Are those clothes the clothes I wore?
Are those skies the skies I saw?
Those the hills that round me ranged?
Is it me or they have changed?

Did Auntie Gwladys wear that hat?
What made Beryl smile like that?
Why is Eileen staring right?
What was happening out of sight?

What the dreams that filled our heads?
What the words that once were said?
What would *he* I used to be
If he met *me* think of me?

Real Life

'Yes,' thought John
his eyes gleaming with excitement
as he looked round the ancient Inn
on the edge of the moors
that was connected to
otherwise inaccessible St Peter's Cove
which had once been a haunt of smugglers
by a secret underground passage
from his bedroom
and which his strange Aunt Lucy
had rented to his mother and father
and Uncle David for
the whole summer holidays.
'Yes, this looks just the sort
of place for an adventure but
that kind of thing
only happens in books.'
And he was right.

Ping-Pong

Swatted between bats
The celluloid ball
Leaps on unseen elastic
Skimming the taut net

Sliced		Spun
Screwed		Cut
Dabbed		Smashed
	Point	
	Service	
Ping		Pong
Pong		Ping
Bing		Bong
Bong		Bing
	Point	
	Service	
Ding		Dong
Dong		Ding
Ting		Tong
Tang		Tong
	Point	
	Service	
Angled		Slipped
Cut		Driven
Floated		Caressed
Driven		Hammered
	THWACKED	
	Point	
	Service	

Bit		Bat
Tip		Tap
Slip		Slap
Zip		Zap
Whip		Whap
	Point	
	Service	
Left		Yes
Right		Yes
Twist		Yes
Skids		Yes
Eighteen		Seventeen
Eighteen		All
Nineteen		Eighteen
Nineteen		All
Twenty		Nineteen
	Point	
	Service	
Forehand		Backhand
Swerves		Yes
Rockets		Yes
Battered		Ah
Cracked		Ah

SMASHED

SMASHED

SMASHED

GAME

The Stomach Ache

Somebody is in there
Where I can't reach,
Somebody with a grudge
And a knowledge of torture,
Some evil thing
Who sups on suffering,
Someone whose yellow fingers
Knead and plunge,
Someone who smiles
And while he smiles
Screws up my innards
In malicious knots,
Someone with eyes tight closed
And wrinkles on his flesh,
Someone who pummels with his bony elbows,
Gurgles with green glee
Stamps his boots about
And starts to suck me
Through his broken teeth
Swallowing me, inside out.

Sitting on Trev's back wall on the last day of the holidays trying to think of something to do

We sit and squint on Trev's back wall
By the clothes line
Watching the shirts flap
Hearing the shirts slap
In the sunshine.
There's nothing much to do at all
But try to keep cool
And it's our last day
Of the holiday
Tomorrow we're back at school.

We keep suggesting games to play
Like Monopoly
But you need a day
If you want to play
It properly.
We played for four hours yesterday
Between rainfalls
In Trev's front room
That's like a tomb
And always smells of mothballs.

Says Trev, 'Why don't we kick a ball
Over the Wasteground?'
But the weather's got
Far too hot
To run around.

John kicks his heels against the wall
Stokesey scratches his head
I head a ball
Chalk my name on the wall
While Trev pretends that he's dead.

Says John, 'Let's go to the cinder track
And play speedway.
We can go by the dykes
It's not far on our bikes
I'll lead the way.'
'My saddlebag's all straw at the back
Being used by blackbirds.'
'And there's something unreal
About my fixed wheel
It only drives me backwards.'

Trev's Granny chucks out crusts of bread
For the sparrows
While their black cat
Crouches flat
Winking in the shadows.
Trev leaps up and bangs his head
With a sudden roar.
'We could er . . .' he says.
'We could er . . .' he says.
And then sits down once more.

'Let's play Releevo on the sands,'
Says John at last.
We set out with a shout
But his mother calls out,
'It's gone half past
Your tea's all laid, you wash your hands
They're absolutely grey.'
'Oh go on Mum
Do I have to come
We were just going out to play.'

Old Stokes trails home and pulls a face,
'I'll see you Trev.'
'See you John.'
'See you Trev.'
'See you tonight the usual place.'
'Yes right, all right.'
'Don't forget.'
'You bet.'
'See you then tonight.'
'See you.'
'See you.'
'See
You.'

Empty House

There is nothing
Quite so dismal
As an empty house;
The door bell's clangour
Tears apart the silence
Rousing no one.
Nothing moves;
Not a sound
Save the chasing echoes
And the clock's hollow
Tock, tock
Measuring the emptiness;
Behind the frosted door
No friendly, welcome shadow looms,
No footsteps cross the floor.

The yellow key
Hides coldly in its hiding place
Behind the rusty carcass of the BSA
Amongst old tins of paint;
Maps of oil stain the floor
And in the air
The smell of dust, turps, sawdust
(Property of all garages).
Whistling softly,
I turn the key
And open the door slowly
As if the emptiness
Was a stranger
I might find sitting
Silent in an armchair.

The house is strange,
Not mine any more,
Holding its breath,
Waiting; a house not real,
Not itself
But an accurate copy taken from life,
Familiar but lacking warmth.
The note from mother
Telling me not to let the fire go out
Scrawled on an envelope
Leans against the clock.
I wander through deserted rooms
Touching familiar objects,
Comforted by companionable flowers in a jar
And by the bulk of our white cat
Who dozes on whatever.

The coals have crumbled to ash;
The fire is out.
I lie, my feet up on a chair,
Reading my comic,
Wishing my mother could be home
To tell me not to put them there.

Unemployable

'I usth thu workth in the thircusth,'
He said,
Between the intermittent showers that
emerged from his mouth.
'Oh,' I said, 'what did you do?'
'I usth thu catcth bulleth in my theeth.'

The Fight

The kick off is
I don't like him;
Nothing about him.
He's fat and soft;
Like a jellybaby he is.
Now he's never done nothing,
Not to me,
He wouldn't dare:
Nothing at all of anything like that.
I just can't stand him,
So I'll fight him
And I'll beat him,
I could beat him any day.

The kick off is it's his knees:
They knock together,
They sock together.
And they're fat,
With veins that run into his socks
Too high.
Like a girl he is,
And his shorts,
Too long,
They look
All wrong,
Like a Mum's boy.
Then
He simpers and dimples,
Like a big lass he is;
So I'll fight him
Everyone beats him,
I could beat him any day.

For another thing it's his hair,
All smarmed and oily fair,
All silk and parted flat,
His mum does it like that
With her flat hand and water,
All licked and spittled into place,
With the quiff all down his face.
And his satchel's new
With his name in blue
Chalked on it.
So I chalked on it,
'Trevor is a cissie'
On it.
So he's going to fight me,
But I'll beat him,
I could beat him any day.

There's a crowd behind the sheds
When we come they turn their heads
Shouting and laughing,
Wanting blood and a bashing.
Take off my coat, rush him,
Smash him, bash him
Lash him, crash him
In the head,
In the bread
Basket.
Crack, thwack,
He's hit me back
Shout and scream

'Gerroff me back,
Gerroff, gerroff!
You wait, I'll get you,
I could beat you any day!'

Swing punch, bit his hand.
Blood on teeth, blood on sand.
Buttons tear, shouts and sighs,
Running nose, tears in eyes.

I'll get him yet; smack him yet.
Smash his smile, teacher's pet.
Brow grazed by knuckle
Knees begin to buckle.
'Gerroff me arms you're hurtin' me!'
'Give in?'
'No.'
'Give in?'
'No. Gerroff me arms!'
'Give in?'
'No.'
'Give in?'
'GIVE IN?'
'NEVER.'
'GIVE IN?'
'OOOH GERROFF GERROFF.'
'GIVE IN?'
'I . . . give . . . in . . . yeah.'

Don't cry, don't cry,
Wipe tears from your eye.
Walk home all alone
In the gutters all alone.

Next time I'll send him flying,
I wasn't really trying;
I could beat him any day.

Winter Days

Biting air
Winds blow
City streets
Under snow

Noses red
Lips sore
Runny eyes
Hands raw

Chimneys smoke
Cars crawl
Piled snow
On garden wall

Slush in gutters
Ice in lanes
Frosty patterns
On window panes

Morning call
Lift up head
Nipped by winter
Stay in bed

Friday Morning Last Two Lessons is Games Day

We straggle in twos
Down Endbutt Lane to the playing fields
In a gap-toothed murmuring line
Filling the pavement.
Mr Pearson strides out in front
The ball tucked firmly under one arm,
His head bent.

We avoid lamp posts
And young mothers pushing prams,
Sometimes walk gammy-legged in gutters
Or scuffle through damp leaves.
The morning is filled
With laughter-tongued and pottering mongrels;
Old men tending bare borders
Slowly unbend
And lean upon their brooms to watch us pass.
Their wives in flowered pinnies
Peer through the lace curtains
Of unused front rooms.

At the pitch
We change in the old pavilion
That smells of dust and feet
And has knot holes in the boarding.

Someone
From another class
Has left
One
Blue and white sock behind.
The lads shout about other games
And goals and saves and shots
Or row about who'll wear red or blue.
Pearson blows exasperation
Briskly through his whistle,
'Come on lads, let's be having you.'

With eighteen a side
We tear after the ball shouting,
Longing to give it a good clean belt,
Perform some piece of perfection –
Beat three sprawling backs in a mazy dribble,
Race full pelt onto a plate-laid-on pass
And crack it full of hate and zest
Past the diving goalie to bulge the net.
But there is no net
And we have to leg it after the ball
To the allotments by the lane
Before we can take centre
To start the game again.

Afterwards,
Still wearing football socks,
Studded boots slung on my shoulder,
I say 'Tarrah' to Trev
At Station Road and drift home
Playing the game again.
Smoke climbs steep from neat red chimneys;
Babies drool and doze
And laugh at the empty sky.
There is the savour of cabbage and gravy
About the Estate and the flowers do not hear
The great crowd roaring me on.

Street Boy

Just you look at me, man,
Stompin' down the street
My crombie stuffed with biceps
My boots is filled with feet.

Just you hark to me, man,
When they call us out
My head is full of silence
My mouth is full of shout.

Just you watch me move, man,
Steady like a clock
My heart is spaced on blue beat
My soul is stoned on rock.

Just you read my name, man,
Writ for all to see
The walls is red with stories
The streets is filled with me.

Friends

When first I went to school
I walked with Sally.
She carried my lunch pack,
Told me about a book she'd read
With a handsome hero
So I said,
'You be my best friend.'
After break I went right off her.
I can't say why
And anyway I met Joan
Who's pretty with dark curls
And we sat in a corner of the playground
And giggled about the boy who brought the milk.
Joan upset me at lunch,
I can't remember what she said actually,
But I was definitely upset
And took up with Hilary
Who's frightfully brilliant and everything
And showed me her history
Which I considered very decent.
The trouble with Hilary is
She has to let you know how clever she is
And I said,
'You're not the only one who's clever you know,'
And she went all quiet and funny
And hasn't spoken to me since.
Good riddance I say
And anyway Linda is much more my type of girl;
She does my hair in plaits

And says how pretty I look,
She really says what she thinks
And I appreciate that.
Nadine said she was common
When we saw her on the bus that time
Sitting with three boys from that other school,
And I had to agree
There was something in what she said.
There's a difference between friendliness
And being cheap
And I thought it my duty
To tell her what I thought.
Well she laughed right in my face
And then pretended I wasn't there
So I went right off her.
If there's one thing I can't stand
It's being ignored and laughed at.
Nadine understood what I meant,
Understood right away
And that's jolly nice in a friend.
I must tell you one thing about her,
She's rather a snob.
I get the feeling
She looks down on me
And she'll never come to my house
Though I've asked her thousands of times.
I thought it best to have it out with her
And she went off in a huff
Which rather proved my point
And I considered myself well rid.

At the moment
I walk home on my own
But I'm keeping my eyes open
And when I see somebody I consider suitable
I'll befriend her.

Moggy in the City

Old fat moggy
Padding on grimy cobbles
Slouching past washing
Rooting in dustbins
Picking your way past puddles
Gliding down ginnels
Miaowling on walls
Purring and rubbing
Round mothers and prams
Rambling through rubbish heaps
Crouching in old cars
Treading the streets
Of dirty old Mother Liverpool.
You,
I feel,
Deserved more
But you betray no resentment
In slow-closing eyes
And somehow with stripes
And regal softness
Make our city better.

A Stomach Ache is Worse Away from Home

'Sir,' I said,
Hoping for sympathy,
'I've got the stomach ache.'
All of it was true,
There was no putting it on.
I gave out winces with my mouth
Using my eyebrows skilfully
And held the hurt place hard
With both hands.
But it was my white face convinced him.
So he sent me outside
To walk it away in the fresh air.
Outside it was deathly cold.
Because he had his hand up first
Trev came out too
To see I was all right.
A grey wind with rain in it
Whipped across the playground,
Spattering through puddles
And setting the empties rolling
Up and down, up and down
And clatter-rattling in their crates.
Trev said, 'You'll be all right.'
And started kicking a tennis ball
Up against the toilet wall,
His hands in his pockets,
Bent against the cold.

The dinner ladies came out.
Moaning slightly I bent over
And gritted my teeth bravely.
But they didn't see
And walked through the school gates laughing.
At home there would be the smell of cooking
And our Robbo asleep before the fire.
I looked through the railings
And thought my way to our house.
Past the crumbling wall,
The Bingo Hall,
The scraggy tree
As thin as me,
The rotting boarding
By the cinema
With last week's star
In a Yankee car
Flapping on the hoarding.
Stop!
Turn right towards town
And three doors down,
That's our house.

The Wind

Listen to the wind awailing
Rattling the garden gate
Brushing the leaves of the oak tree
Rustling in the grate.

The cat lies flat on the hearth rug
Washing his face with his paws
The dog's asleep in the basket
Everyone's indoors.

It screams along the alleys
It bellows up the street
It groans between the gravestones
It bowls hats along the street.

It's pounding at the windows
Like the hooves of an angry horse
If it blows like this much longer
It'll knock the world off its course.

It's quietened down at bedtime
Snoring loud and deep
At six it rattles the milk crates
And finally falls asleep.

Hymn to the Twentieth Century

Give me a new Ford car around me,
Four Goodyear tyres below,
And Belsize undersealing
To protect me from the snow.

Give me High Speed Gas to warm me,
And Slumbertight by night,
Venetian blinds by Windofurn
To filter in the light.

Let the telly be my window
On all that lives without,
And my Dina pop transistor
Beat the silence out.

Give me beef steaks made in factories,
Potatoes grown in tins,
Let the Welfare State that loves me
Expiate my sins.

Let my shirt be made of Nusilk,
That cost the worm no sleep,
And the pile on my Woolies' sweater
Be clipped from synthetic sheep.

The plastic flowers in my garden
Have a brightness that can't be ignored,
And the lawn just never needs cutting
When it's sown by Cyril Lord.

Don't kick the second millennium,
Don't let it make you feel low,
Just make the best of what you've got,
There's nowhere else you can go.

Bedroom Skating

Because there is no Ice Rink
Within fifty miles of our house,
My sister perfects her dance routines
In the Olympic Stadium of my bedroom.
Wearing a soft expression
And two big, yellow dusters on her feet,
She explodes out of cupboards
To an avalanche of music
And whirls about the polished lino
In a blur of double axels and triple salchows.
For her free-style doubles
She hurls this pillow called Torvill
From here to breakfast-time
While spinning like a hippo
Round and round my bed.
Imagine waking up to that each morning;
Small wonder my hands shake
And I'm off my cornflakes.
Last Thursday she even made me
Stand up on my bed
And hold up cards marked 'Six'
While she gave victory salutes
In the direction of the gerbil's cage.
To be honest,
Despite her endless dedication
And her hours of practice
I don't think she has a hope
Of lifting the world title.
But who cares?

She may not get the gold
But I'll bet there isn't another skater alive
With wall-to-wall mirror
On her bedroom floor.

Drama Lesson

'Let's see some super shapes you Blue Group,'
Mr Lavender shouts down the hall.
'And forests don't forget your trembly leaves
And stand up straight and tall.'

But Phillip Chubb is in our group
And he wants to be Robin Hood
And Ann Boot is sulking because she's not with her friend
And I don't see why I should be wood.

The lights are switched on in the classrooms,
Outside the sky's nearly black,
And the dining-hall smells of gravy and fat
And Chubb has boils down his back.

Sir tells him straight that he's got to be tree
But he won't wave his arms around.
'How can I wave my branches, Sir,
Friar Tuck has chopped them all down.'

Then I come cantering through Sherwood
To set Maid Marian free
And I really believe I'm Robin Hood
And the Sheriff's my enemy.

At my back my trusty longbow
My broadsword clanks at my side,
My outlaws gallop behind me
As into adventure we ride.

'Untie that maid you villain,' I shout
With all the strength I have,
But the tree has got bored and is picking his nose
And Maid Marian has gone to the lav.

After rehearsals, Sir calls us together
And each group performs their play,
But just as it comes to our turn
The bell goes for the end of the day.

As I trudge my way home through the city streets
The cars and the houses retreat
And a thunder of hooves beats in my mind
And I gallop through acres of wheat.

The castle gleams white in the distance,
The banners flap, golden and red,
And distant trumpets weave silver dreams
In the landscape of my head.

Uncle Alfred's Long Jump

When Mary Rand
Won the Olympic Long Jump,
My Auntie Hilda
Paced out the distance
On the pavement outside her house.
'Look at that!'
She shouted challengingly
At the dustman, the milkman, the grocer,
Two Jehovah's Witnesses
And a male St Bernard
Who happened to be passing,
'A girl, a girl did that;
If you men are so clever
Let's see what you can do.'
Nobody took up the challenge
Until Uncle Alfred trudged home
Tired from the office
Asking for his tea.
'Our Mary did that!'
Said Auntie Hilda proudly
Pointing from the lamp post
To the rose bush by her gate.
'You men are so clever,
Let's see how near
That rose bush you end up.'
His honour and manhood at stake,
Uncle Alfred put down his bowler
His briefcase and his brolly
And launched himself
Into a fifty yard run-up.

'End up at that rose bush,'
He puffed mockingly,
'I'll show you where I'll end up.'
His take-off from the lamp post
Was a thing of beauty,
But where he ended up
Was in The Royal Infirmary
With both legs in plaster.
'Some kind of record!'
He said proudly to the bone specialist;
While through long nights
In a ward full of coughs and snoring
He dreamed about the washing line
And of how to improve
His high jump technique.

The Ghoul

One dark and wintry evening
When snow swirled through the air
And the wind howled like a banshee
I crept silently up the stair.

I sat in the quiet of my bedroom
And opened with bated breath
My *Zombie Horror Make-Up Kit*
That would frighten my sister to death.

Slowly my face began to change
As I carefully applied the pack,
I laughed at my face in the mirror
But an evil stranger leered back.

Long hair sprouted wild from my forehead,
My nose was half snout, half beak,
My right eye bulged angry and bloodshot
While the left crawled over my cheek.

My fangs hung low and broken,
My chin was cratered with sores,
The backs of my hands were mats of hair,
My fingers grew long, bird-like claws.

Heard my sister's key in the front door,
Heard her calling, 'Anyone in?'
Took a long, last look at the thing in the glass,
Distorted and ugly as sin.

My sister was running the water,
She sang as she washed her hair,
I heard her call out as a floorboard creaked,
'Hello, is anyone there?'

And then I released my zombie howl
As I crashed through the kitchen door,
I caught sight of a ghoul in the window pane
And passed out cold on the floor.

Den to Let

To let
One self-contained
Detached den.
Accommodation is compact
Measuring one yard square.
Ideal for two eight-year-olds
Plus one small dog
Or two cats
Or six gerbils.
Accommodation consists of:
One living-room
Which doubles as kitchen
Bedroom
Entrance-hall
Dining-room
Dungeon
Space capsule
Pirate boat
Covered wagon
Racing car
Palace
Aeroplane
Junk-room
And look-out post.
Property is southward facing
And can be found
Within a short walking distance
Of the back door
At bottom of garden.

Easily found in the dark
By following the smell
Of old cabbages and tea-bags.
Convenient escape routes
Past rubbish dump
To Seager's Lane
Through hole in hedge,
Or into next door's garden;
But beware of next door's rhinoceros
Who sometimes thinks he's a poodle.
Construction is of
Sound corrugated iron
And roof doubles as shower
During rainy weather.
Being partially underground,
Den makes
A particularly effective hiding place
When in a state of war
With older sisters
Brothers
Angry neighbours
Or when you simply want to be alone.
Some repair work needed
To north wall
Where Mr Spence's foot came through
When planting turnips last Thursday.
With den go all contents
Including:
One carpet – very smelly
One teapot – cracked
One woolly penguin –
No beak and only one wing

One unopened tin
Of sultana pud
One hundred and three Beanos
Dated 1983–1985
And four Rupert annuals.
Rent is free
The only payment being
That the new occupant
Should care for the den
In the manner to which it has been accustomed
And on long Summer evenings
Heroic songs of days gone by
Should be loudly sung
So that old and glorious days
Will never be forgotten.

Are You There Moriarty?

None of my aunties
Cared much for Uncle Arthur.
Somewhere deep down
Where auntiness is bred
They thought of him as evil
And worse than that ill-mannered.
He dredged his tea out of a saucer
Through the yellow sieve of his great moustache;
Removed his boots in mixed company
And smoked a huge curved pipe
That smelled of condemned socks.
Sometimes, when contemplation took him,
He'd chuckle to himself at private
And disreputable thoughts
And gob a stream of thick brown juice
With sizzling accuracy
Into the heart of the fire.
Arthur wasn't the stuff
That aunts are made of
But if you were under twelve
And relished blood and dirt
Uncle Arthur was magic!
He could wiggle his ears till the cows came home,
Belch thunderously at will
And produce streams of soft-boiled eggs
From either nostril.
At Christmas he came into his own:
Between the turkey and the pudding
He'd play a game of billiards
With his glass eye and a kitchen knife

Shouting, 'Pot the red!'
At screaming Auntie Muriel
As the eye dropped into her lap.
For his piece de resistance
He'd remove his huge false teeth
And make them sing
God Save the King
As he tapped the rhythm out
With fervour on the spoons.
Then after dinner,
When the aunts retired to the parlour
To snooze and share their disapproving clucks,
Uncle Arthur would draw the blinds,
Turn out the lights
And tell us harrowing tales
Of headless, bloodstained men
Who flew down children's chimneys
And performed such hideous deeds
The girls had nightmares into March,
While Cousin Edgar,
Who was sensitive
And pressed wild flowers,
Wet the bed until his dying day.
When only the strong remained,
We'd play Uncle Arthur's favourite game
'Are you there Moriarty?'
Which involved a string of juvenile challengers
Lying blindfold on their stomachs
And screaming out the challenge
While trying to knock each other senseless
With rolled-up copies of *The Echo*.

Now, whenever I pass the cemetery
Where Uncle Arthur long lies buried,
I think of him,
Stretched out upon a marble slab,
His great pipe pouring smoke,
Spitting thoughtfully between his socks
And laughing at us all.
And for his sake I call,
Too quiet I know for Uncle Arthur's taste,
'Are you there Moriarty?'
And it seems to me
That from far away
I hear a rolled-up paper crashing down
On some unfortunate skull
And from somewhere
Deep in Death's chill parlour
Comes the kind of sound
That disapproving aunts would make
If they could ruffle their feathers.

Conversation Piece

Late again Blenkinsop?
What's the excuse this time?
Not my fault sir.
Whose fault is it then?
Grandma's sir.
Grandma's. What did she do?
She died sir.
Died?
She's seriously dead all right sir.
That makes four grandmothers this term
And all on PE days Blenkinsop.
I know. It's very upsetting sir.
How many grandmothers have you got Blenkinsop?
Grandmothers sir? None sir.
None?
All dead sir.
And what about yesterday Blenkinsop?
What about yesterday sir?
You missed maths.
That was the dentist sir.
The dentist died?
No sir. My teeth sir.
You missed the test Blenkinsop.
I'd been looking forward to it too sir.
Right, line up for PE.
Can't sir.
No such word as can't. Why can't you?
No kit sir.
Where is it?
Home sir.

What's it doing at home?
Not ironed sir.
Couldn't you iron it?
Can't do it sir.
Why not?
My hand sir.
Who usually does it?
Grandma sir.
Why couldn't she do it?
Dead sir.

Name Poem

Borg and Best and Geoffrey Boycott,
Marvellous Marvin, Little Mo,
Graeme Souness, Peter Shilton,
Johan Cruyff, Sebastian Coe.

Steve Ovett and Olga Korbut,
Willie Carson, Raymond Floyd,
Kevin Keegan, Trevor Brooking,
Zola Budd, Chris Evert-Lloyd.

Joel Garner, Arnold Palmer,
Barry John, Torvill and Dean,
Nel Tarlton, Bobby Charlton,
Vivian Richards, Barry Sheene.

Navratilova, Betty Stove,
Di Stefano, Denis Law,
Botham, Willey, Dennis Lillee,
Muhammad Ali, Garry Shaw.

Charlie Nicholas, Jack Nicklaus,
Joe Louis, Sugar Ray,
Zico, Faldo, Pelé, Falcoã,
Michael Holding, Andy Gray.

Franz Klammer, David Gower,
Sharron Davies, Terry Paine,
Whirlwind White and Giant Haystacks,
Alex Higgins the Hurricane.

Dear Examiner

Thank you so much for your questions
I've read them all carefully through
But there isn't a single one of them
That I know the answer to.

I've written my name as instructed
Put the year, the month and the day
But after I'd finished doing that
I had nothing further to say.

So I thought I'd write you a letter
Fairly informally
About what's going on in the classroom
And what it's like to be me.

Mandy has written ten pages
But it's probably frightful guff
And Angela Smythe is copying
The answers off her cuff.

Miss Quinlan is marking our homework
The clock keeps ticking away
For anyone not in this classroom
It's just another day.

Mother's buying groceries
Grandmother's drinking tea
Unemployed men doing crosswords
Or watching *Crown Court* on TV.

The drizzle has finally stopped here
The sun's just started to shine
And in a back garden in Sefton Road
A housewife hangs shirts on the line.

A class chatters by to play tennis
The cathedral clock has just pealed
A motor chugs steadily back and forth
Mowing the hockey field.

Miss Quinlan's just seen what I've written
Her face is an absolute mask
Before she collects in the papers
I have one little favour to ask.

I thought your questions were lovely
There's only myself to blame
But couldn't you give me something
For writing the date and my name?

Time Child

Dandelion, dandelion,
Dandelion flower,
If I breathe upon thee
Pray tell me the hour.

Little child, little child,
Little child I pray,
Breathe but gently on me
Lest you blow the time away.

Song of the City

The Owl and the Astronaut

The owl and the astronaut
Sailed through space
In their intergalactic ship
They kept hunger at bay
With three pills a day
And drank through a protein drip.
The owl dreamed of mince
And slices of quince
And remarked how life had gone flat;
'It may be all right
To fly faster than light
But I preferred the boat and the cat.'

Thoughts like an Ocean

The sea comes to me on the shore
On lacy slippered feet
And shyly, slyly slides away
With a murmur of defeat.

And as I stand there wondering
Strange thoughts spin round my head
Of why and where and what and when
And if not, why, what then?

Where do lobsters come from?
And where anemones?
And are there other worlds out there
With other mysteries?

Why do *I* walk upon dry land
While fishes haunt the sea?
And as I think about their lives
Do they too think of me?

Why is water, water?
Why does it wet my hand?
Are there really as many stars
As there are grains of sand?

And where would the ocean go to
If there were no gravity?
And where was I before I lived?
And where's eternity?

Perhaps the beach I'm standing on
Perhaps this stretch of sand
Perhaps the Universe itself
Lies on someone else's hand?

And isn't it strange how this water and I
At this moment happened to meet
And how this tide sweeps half the world
Before stopping at my feet.

Come on in the Water's Lovely

Come on in the water's lovely
It isn't really cold at all
Of course you'll be quite safe up this end
If you hold tight to the wall.

Of course that fat boy there won't drown you
He's too busy drowning Gail
Just imagine you're a tadpole.
I *know* you haven't got a tail.

Oh come on in the water's lovely
Warm and clear as anything
All the bottom tiles are squiggly
And your legs like wriggly string.

Come on in the water's lovely
It's no good freezing on the side
How do you know you're going to drown
Unless you've really tried.

What? You're really going to do it?
You'll jump in on the count of three?
Of course the chlorine doesn't blind you
Dive straight in and you'll soon see.

One – it isn't really deep at all.
Two – see just comes to my chin.
Three – oh there's the bell for closing time
And just as you jumped in!

Typewriting Class

Dear Miss Hinson
I am spitting
In front of my top ratter
With the rest of my commercesnail sturdy students
Triping you this later.
The truce is Miss Hinson
I am not hippy wiht my cross.
Every day on Woundsday
I sit in my dusk
With my type rutter
Trooping without lurking at the lattice
All sorts of weird messengers.
To give one exam pill,
'The quick down socks . . .
The quick brine pox . . .
The sick frown box . . .
The sick down jocks
Humps over the hazy bog'
When everyone knows
That a sick down jock
Would not be seen dead
Near a hazy bog.
Another one we tripe is;
'Now is the tame
For all guide men
To cram to the head
Of the pratty.'
To may why of sinking
If that is all you get to tripe
In true whelks of sturdy

Then I am thinking of changing
To crookery crasses.
I would sooner end up a crook
Than a shirt hand trappist
Any die of the wink.
I have taken the tremble, Miss Hinson
To tripe you this later
So that you will be able
To underhand my indignation.
I must clothe now
As the Bill is groaning

> Yours fitfully . . .

Miss Creedle Teaches Creative Writing

'This morning,' cries Miss Creedle,
'We're all going to use our imaginations,
We're going to close our eyes 3W and imagine.
Are we ready to imagine Darren?
I'm going to count to three.
At one, we wipe our brains completely clean;
At two, we close our eyes;
And at three, we imagine.
Are we all imagining? Good.
Here is a piece of music by Beethoven to help us.
Beethoven's dates were 1770 to 1827.
(See The Age of Revolutions in your History books.)
Although Beethoven was deaf and a German
He wrote many wonderful symphonies,
But this was a long time before anyone of us was born.
Are you imagining a time before you were born?
What does it look like? Is it dark?
(Embryo is a good word you might use.)
Does the music carry you away like a river?
What is the name of the river? Can you smell it?
Foetid is an exciting adjective.
As you float down the river
Perhaps you land on an alien planet.
Tell me what sounds you hear.
If there are indescribable monsters
Tell me what they look like but not now.
(Your book entitled *Tackle Pre-History This Way*
Will be of assistance here.)
Perhaps you are cast adrift in a broken barrel

In stormy shark-infested waters
(Remember the work we did on piranhas for RE?)
Try to see yourself. Can you do that?
See yourself at the bottom of a pothole in the Andes
With both legs broken
And your life ebbing away inexorably.
What does the limestone feel like?
See the colours.
Have you done that? Good.
And now you may open your eyes.
Your imagining time is over,
Now it is writing time.
Are we ready to write? Good.
Then write away.
Wayne, you're getting some exciting ideas down.
Tracy, that's lovely.
Darren, you haven't written anything.
Couldn't you put the date?
You can't think of anything to write.
Well, what did you see when you closed your eyes?
But you must have seen something beside the black.
Yes, apart from the little squiggles.
Just the black. I see.
Well, try to think
Of as many words for black as you can.'

Miss Creedle whirls about the class
Like a benign typhoon
Spinning from one quailing homestead to another.
I dream of peaceful ancient days
In Mr Swindell's class
When the hours passed like a dream
Filled with order and measuring and tests.

Excitement is not one of the things I come to school for.
I force my eyes shut
But all I see
Is a boy of twelve
Sitting at a desk one dark November day
Writing this poem.
And Darren is happy to discover
There is only one word for black
And that will have to suffice
Until the bell rings for all of us.

Out in the City

When you're out in the city
Shuffling down the street,
A bouncy city rhythm
Starts to boogie in your feet.

It jumps off the pavement,
There's a snare drum in your brain,
It pumps through your heart
Like a diesel train.

There's Harry on the corner,
Sings, 'How she goin' boy?'
To loose and easy Winston
With his brother Leroy.

Shout, 'Hello!' to Billy Brisket
With his tripes and cows' heels,
Blood-stained rabbits
And trays of live eels.

Maltese Tony
Smoking in the shade
Keeping one good eye
On the amusement arcade.

And everybody's talking:

Move along
Step this way
Here's a bargain
What you say?
Mind your backs
Here's your stop
More fares?
Room on top.

Neon lights and take-aways
Gangs of boys and girls
Football crowds and market stalls
Taxi cabs and noise.

From the city cafes
On the smoky breeze
Smells of Indian cooking
Greek and Cantonese.

Well, some people like suburban life
Some people like the sea
Others like the countryside
But it's the city
Yes it's the city
It's the city life
For me.

The Commentator

Good afternoon and welcome
To this international
Between England and Holland
Which is being played here today
At 4, Florence Terrace.
And the pitch looks in superb condition
As Danny Markey, the England captain,
Puts England on the attack.
Straight away it's Markey
With a lovely little pass to Keegan,
Keegan back to Markey,
Markey in possession here
Jinking skilfully past the dustbins;
And a neat flick inside the cat there.
What a brilliant player this Markey is
And he's still only nine years old!
Markey to Francis,
Francis back to Markey,
Markey is through, he's through,
No, he's been tackled by the drainpipe;
But he's won the ball back brilliantly
And he's advancing on the Dutch keeper,
It must be a goal.
The keeper's off his line
But Markey chips him superbly
And it's a goal
No!
It's gone into Mrs Spence's next door.
And Markey's going round to ask for his ball back,
It could be the end of this international.

Now the door's opening
And yes, it's Mrs Spence,
Mrs Spence has come to the door.
Wait a minute
She's shaking her head, she is shaking her head,
She's not going to let England have their ball back.
What is the referee going to do?
Markey's coming back looking very dejected,
And he seems to be waiting . . .
He's going back,
Markey is going back for that ball!
What a brilliant and exciting move!
He waited until the front door was closed
And then went back for that ball.
And wait a minute,
He's found it, Markey has found that ball,
He has found that ball
And that's wonderful news
For the hundred thousand fans gathered here
Who are showing their appreciation
In no uncertain fashion.
But wait a minute,
The door's opening once more.
It's her, it's Mrs Spence
And she's waving her fist
And shouting something I can't quite understand
But I don't think it's encouragement.
And Markey's off,
He's jinked past her on the outside
Dodging this way and that
With Mrs Spence in hot pursuit.
And he's past her, he's through,
What skills this boy has!

But Mr Spence is there too,
Mr Spence in the sweeper role
With Rover their dog.
Markey's going to have to pull out all the stops now.
He's running straight at him,
And he's down, he's down on all fours!
What is he doing?
And Oh my goodness that was brilliant,
That was absolutely brilliant,
He's dived through Spence's legs;
But he's got him,
This rugged stopper has him by the coat
And Rover's barking in there too;
He'll never get out of this one.
But this is unbelievable!
He's got away
He has got away:
He wriggled out of his coat
And left part of his trousers with Rover.
This boy is real dynamite.
He's over the wall
He's clear
They'll never catch him now.
He's down the yard and on his way
And I don't think we're going to see
Any more of Markey
Until it's safe to come home.

The New House

I don't much like this bedroom
The bedroom doesn't like me
It looks like a sort of policeman
Inspecting a refugee.

I don't like the look of the bathroom
It's just an empty space
And the mirror seems used to staring at
A completely different face.

I don't like the smell of the kitchen
And the garden wet with rain
It feels like an empty station
Where I'm waiting for a train.

I can't kick a ball against this wall,
I can't build a house in this tree
And the streets are as quiet and deserted
As the local cemetery.

I don't like the look of the kids next door
Playing in the beat-up car
Why do they stand and stare at me?
Who do they think they are?

The big boy's coming over
He's just about my height
Why has he got a brick in his hand?
Is he going to pick a fight?

But he asks me into their garden
Tells me his name is Ben
And Jane is the name of his sister
And will I help build their den.

We can't get it finished by dinner
We won't get it finished by tea
But there's plenty of time in the days ahead
For Ben and for Jane and for me.

Street Cricket

On August evenings by the lamp post
When the days are long and light
The lads come out for cricket
And play until it's night.
They bat and bowl and field and shout
And someone shouts 'HOWZAT!'
But you can't give Peter Batty out
Or he'll take away his bat.

The dogs in the Close all love to field
And chase about the street
The stumper wears his mother's gloves
And stops the ball with his feet.
Everyone should have a bowl
That's the proper way to play
But Batty has to bowl all night
Or he takes his ball away.

When lamps and rooms turn on their lights
And you can hardly see the ball
The lads begin to drift off home
You can hear the goodbyes they call.
But Peter Batty's two hundred not out
And he shouts as he walks away,
'Remember I'm batting tomorrow night
Or I won't let anyone play.'

Half Asleep

Half asleep
And half awake
I drift like a boat
On an empty lake.
And the sounds in the house
And the street that I hear
Though far away sound very clear.
That's my sister Betty
Playing by the stairs
Shouting like teacher
At her teddy bears.
I can hear Mum chatting
To the woman next door
And the tumble dryer
Vibrates through the floor.
That's Alan Simpson
Playing guitar
While his Dad keeps trying
To start their car.
Dave the mechanic
Who's out on strike
Keeps revving and tuning
His Yamaha bike.
From the open window
Across the street
On the August air
Drifts a reggae beat.
At four o'clock
With a whoop and a shout
The kids from St John's

Come tumbling out.
I can hear their voices
Hear what they say
And I play in my head
All the games that they play.

Bossy Queen Eileen

Out from under a dirty blanket
That she and Betty have slung
Between the rabbit hutch and next door's fence
Come the bossy specs of Bossy Eileen
Followed by her bossy nose
And the rest of her bossy face.
'Bet you'll never guess what we've built,'
Says Bossy Eileen
Tucking her skirt into her knickers
And doing handstands against the wall.
'Is it an Apache tent?' I suggest,
Knowing that whatever I say is bound to be wrong.
Bossy Eileen is just as bossy upside down
As she is the right way up.
'Course not clever clogs so there,'
Says her red upside-down face,
'Anyone can see it's a royal palace.'
Bossy Eileen comes the right way up.
'You must call me Queen Eileen
And your Royal Highness if you want to play,
And this is Princess Betty who's come for tea,'
She says tugging her frock out of her knickers.
'Thank you your majesty,' simpers Betty
Making her thin legs go buckled
And holding up the corners of her skirt.
'If you like,' says Queen Bossy Boots Eileen,
'You can be King today,
Unless you'd rather be a humble footman?'
'No, king will do fine,' I tell her
Curtsying like Betty.

I find out that a king
Spends a lot of time
Bringing rain water in broken plastic cups
And crab apples to the royal tea party.
Betty spoons away at the dirt:
'You must give me the recipe for this junket,'
She says in her put-on voice.
The September afternoon is spent
Sweeping out the battlements,
Bowing to many guests
And rebuilding the royal palace
When the blanket falls in.
So passes
Another royal afternoon.

Bouncing

Sally Arkari isn't she a treat
Bouncing her rubber ball
Up and down the street
Sticking plaster spectacles
Braces on her teeth
Always scoffing chocolates
Always crunching sweets
Never stops bouncing
Wherever she goes
Never stops sniffing
Never blows her nose
She bounces when she's laughing
She bounces when she weeps
She bounces when she's wide awake
She bounces when she sleeps
She bounces in the playground
She bounces in the hall
You can always tell it's Sally
By her bouncing rubber ball
She bounces during Geography
She bounces during Art
She bounces all through dinner time
In the custard tart
She bounces till she's out of breath
And her face turns red
She bounces in assembly
On the teacher's head
She bounces to the fairground
And makes the people cross
As she bounces in the fish and chips

And in the candy floss
She bounces into Paris
And for almost an hour
She bounced her little rubber ball
On the Eiffel Tower
She bounced down to the circus
And up the greasy pole
She bounced down to the football ground
And bounced into the goal
She bounced beside the brass band
As it marched around the town
She bounced among the drummer boys
And made them all fall down
She bounced it on her knee caps
She bounced it on her head
Then she bounced her way back home again
And bounced into her bed.

The Alchemist

There's a mysterious light
Burns all through the night
In that house where some people say
The alchemist dwells
With books full of spells
And a cat who scares children away.

Some say that he lives
In that house all alone
Some say he has claws and a beak
Some say he keeps rats
And vampire bats
And a raven he's taught how to speak.

And the children play dare:
'I dare you to spy
Through the dust on his window pane.'
They say those who dare
To enter his lair
Have never been seen again.

They say that his furnace
Turns iron and bronze
Into ingots of glistening gold.
They say if you take
The powder he makes
You'll never fall sick or grow old.

Some say he's a wizard
Some say he's a saint
Some say he eats toads for his tea
So I don't think I'll pay
Him a visit today
For fear he should want to eat me.

The Cat

Conscious of being a cat
I am given to sensuality.
I like to slide my bulk
Against the nylon ankles of young ladies,
Then again I fold my fur
On silken eiderdowns
And take pleasure in simply walking,
Turn up my nose at meat,
Disdain creamless milk
And fattened by the heat of open fires
Compose myself for sleep
Within the tidy limits of myself
Even in the best company.

The Bantam Cock

Before I cross the farm each day
I always hope and pray
That the green and crimson bantam cock
Won't be there to bar my way.

Oh bantam cock please let me pass
Let me cross your yard today
I beg you please don't charge at me
And make me run away.

Don't make your crop to stand on end
Don't crow your clarion pride
Don't flap your wings and stretch your throat
Don't spread your beak so wide.

I must go fishing in the stream
I just have to cross your farm
I don't intend to steal your eggs
Or cause your chickens harm.

He struts stiff-legged up and down
Like a major on parade
His angry eyes both seem to say
I'm used to being obeyed.

And though I creep so silently
With my rod beneath my arm
He twists his head and lifts his throat
And trumpets his alarm.

Now he's running at me
His head thrust out before
His crimson crop streams in the wind
Like a bloodstained flag of war.

I race across the muddy field
For the safety of the gate
While the bantam comes even closer
On wings of pride and hate.

And just in time I'm safe and sound
And bang the farm gate to
And calmly inform my bristling foe,
'I'm not afraid of you.'

My Sister Betty

My sister Betty said,
'I'm going to be a famous actress.'
Last year she was going to be a missionary.
'Famous actresses always look unhappy but beautiful,'
She said, pulling her mouth sideways
And making her eyes turn upwards
So they were mostly white.
'Do I look unhappy but beautiful?'
'I want to go to bed and read,' I said.
'Famous actresses suffer and have hysterics,' she said.
'I've been practising my hysterics.'
She began going very red and screaming
So that it hurt my ears.
She hit herself on the head with her fists
And rolled off my bed onto the lino.
I stood by the wardrobe where it was safer.
She got up saying, 'Thank you, thank you,'
And bowed to the four corners of my bedroom.
'Would you like an encore of hysterics?' she asked.
'No,' I said from inside the wardrobe.
There was fluff all over her vest.
'If you don't clap enthusiastically,' she said,
'I'll put your light out when you're reading.'
While I clapped a bit
She bowed and shouted, 'More, more!'
Auntie Gwladys shouted upstairs,
'Go to bed and stop teasing our Betty.'
'The best thing about being a famous actress,' Betty said,
'Is that you get to die a lot.'

She fell to the floor with a crash
And lay there for an hour and a half
With her eyes staring at the ceiling.
She only went away when I said,
'You really look like a famous actress
Who's unhappy but beautiful.'

When I got into bed and started reading,
She came and switched off my light.
It's not much fun
Having a famous actress for a sister.

Death of a Gunfighter

Doc Holliday, who are you waiting for
With your fevered eyes alive?
Why do your hands feed cartridges
Into your pearl-handled forty-five?

Doc Holliday, why do you cock an ear
To the hoof beats pattering by?
Who is the stranger on a jet black mare
With death in either eye?

The room throbs like an oven,
The sun climbs up to noon,
The stranger sways in the rocking chair
Outside the Last Chance Saloon.

Doc Holliday asks for a mirror
No reflection in the glass
Only the ghosts of the men he's killed
Smiling as they pass.

The Pinkerton man in Ellsworth
When you were running from the law,
The kid in Dodge out to make his name
By beating you to the draw.

The breed in Butte, Montana,
Who marked you with that scar,
The dude who left a slug in your thigh
From a face out in Wichita.

You can't be searching for glory now
For eternity in the sun
But hoping to find a kind of peace
In the mouth of a stranger's gun.

Doc Holliday white as the sheet on his bed,
The room about him reeled,
Coughed in his white bandanna
Stained like a poppy field.

The stranger sits quiet at the bedside
Watching the life blood spill
Doc's hands reach out for unseen guns
Then slowly flutter still.

The gun belt hangs on the bed post
The hat on a hook on the wall
And the high-heeled boots he'll never wear
Stand polished in the hall.

(Doc Holliday died of tuberculosis in a sanatorium in Glenwood Springs at the age of thirty-five. On his death bed he is reputed to have asked for a last drink of whiskey, then raised his head, looked down at his feet and whispered, 'Well I'll be damned.' Doc had always sworn that he would die with his boots on.)

The Cisco Kid of Cable Street

Down the long dry canyons he rides
Past arroyas and arid gulches lined with mesquite,
Through winding wheels of tumbleweed
Whipped by the hot winds of the sierras
To where amongst the stables
And the clapboard stores
Fate waits for him darkly with feet astride;
Fate who smiles bitterly
And somewhere reserves
A bullet just for him.
Hunched in the saddle
The Kid sings softly
A song about himself and his fame.

>   *'I'm the Cisco Kid of Cable Street,*
>   *My hand moves fast as light.*
>   *In the high noon sun*
>   *I draw my gun*
>   *Fast as a rattler's bite.'*

At the saloon he swings from his palamino,
The hot afternoon holds its breath.
His cool eyes take in the mayor,
The quailing townsfolk frozen in time and fear.
On the threshold of the saloon
He stands motionless;
The hands over the cards hold still
The faro wheel revolves unwatched
The bartender freezes
Amongst the bourbon and the sarsaparilla
His cigar halfway to his lips.
Hands hooked loose over his pearl-handled guns
The Kid walks into his own legend.
'There's your order,'
Says the man behind the counter.
'Tell your mother there's no brown bread today.'
And smiling he hands over the change.
They know not to mess with the Kid.

Horror Film

Well sir, first of all there was this monster
But like he's not really a monster
'Cause in real life he's a bank clerk sir
And sings in this village choir
But he keeps like drinking this potion sir
And you see him like changing into this pig
With black curly hairs on its knuckles;
And what he does sir,
Is he goes round eating people's brains.
Anyway before that sir, I should have said
He's secretly in love with Lady Irene
Who's very rich with lots of long frocks
And she has this identical twin sister
Who looks like her sir
Who keeps getting chased by this monster bulldog
Into these sinking sands
That's inhabited by this prehistoric squid sir
Which like she can't see
Because the deaf and dumb bailiff
With the hump on his back
Has trod on her specs.
Anyway before that sir,
I should have said,
This lady Irene is screaming,
'Henry, Henry, my beloved, save me,'
'Cause she's been walled up in the dripping dungeon
With the mad violinist of the vaults
By the manservant with the withered boot sir.
But this Henry, he can't hear her sir,
Because he's too busy

Putting people in this bubbling acid bath
To make them stay young forever sir
But his experiments keep going wrong.
Anyway, before that sir,
I should have said,
Her Dad can't rescue her either sir
Because of the army of giant ants
That's eating his castle;
And the music sir, it's going,
'Tarrar, tarrar, boom boom tarrar' sir,
And 'Henry, Henry my beloved,'
She keeps screaming
And the mad violinist of the vaults sir
He starts going funny all over the flagstones.
And like, Algernon sir,
No not him sir, the other one,
He can't do nothing about the squid in the bogs
Because he's turning into this pig with hairy knuckles.
Anyway before that sir, I should have said,
There's this huge mummy in the library
And every time he hears this music
Starts tearing off all these dirty bandages
And smashing through these walls and everything
And the professor can't stop him
'Cause he's gone off his rocker
And keeps bulging his eyes and laughing a lot
When suddenly this vampire . . .
Didn't I tell you about the vampire sir?
Anyway before that there's this vampire
Who's been dead for thousands of years
But he's a Swiss greengrocer in real life
But the iceberg his coffin's in
Gets all broken up sir

When it collides with Dr Strenkhoff's submarine sir,
That's carrying this secret cargo
Of radioactive rats . . .
Didn't I tell you about the radioactive rats sir?
Well anyway sir
Before that I should have said . . .

Invalid

Such a commotion
Coming up off the street,
Such a shouting and calling
Such a running of feet.
Such a rolling of marbles
Such a whipping of tops
Such a skipping of skips
Such a hopping of hops –
And I'm in bed.

So much chasing and fighting
Down on the street
Such a claiming of victories
Such howling defeats.
So much punching and shoving
So much threatening to clout
So much running to doorways
Until it's safe to come out –
But I'm in bed.

So much hiding and seeking
From the pavement below
So much argy bargy
Who'll hide and whose go.
Such a throwing of balls
Such picking of sides
Such a racing of bikes
Such a begging of rides –
And I'm in bed.

If I was a dictator
And the world was a street
There'd be no more homework
No school dinners to eat.
I'd abolish exams
I'd banish all sums
And we'd play in a street
Where night never comes –
And I'd never be ill.

Anna Mae 'Chip Shop' O'Sullivan

Anna Mae Chip Shop O'Sullivan
Ran a shop from a Dormobile van.
Served cod wrapped in last week's Beano
Had a chin like Desperate Dan.

Anna Mae Beano O'Sullivan
Built like a battleship
Smoked a pipe like a skull and cross bones
And talked like a comic strip.

She'd say:

JOKE COW PIE FOR THE BASH STREET KIDS
YUK, SPLUTTER, CHOMP AND SPLAT!
GRRR, RAGE, IT'S THAT TOFF LORD SNOOTY
WANTING SPRATS FOR KORKY THE CAT.

Thinks:

THIS SNEEZING SALT SHOULD IMPROVE THE TASTE
ADD SUPERGLUE FLAVOUR FOR FUN
HOHO, CHORTLE CHORTLE WHEN SNITCH AND SNATCH
SCOFF THIS MAGIC EXPLODING BUN.

Moans:

> GROAN, YUK IT'S THAT DENNIS THE MENACE
> EEEK AND WITH GNASHER THE DOG
> OH GLEE THEY'RE SCOFFING THAT HAMBURGER
> STUFFED WITH A YUMMY PLASTIC FROG.

Anna Mae Chip Shop O'Sullivan
Her van wasn't there one day
They said she hadn't a licence
So the council towed her away.

Anna Mae Long Gone O'Sullivan
Your legend won't die though you're gone
You're stored in our dreams like a comic strip
Whose story goes on and on
And on and on
And on

And on

And on

And on

A Dog's Life

Waking up last Friday and dressing for school
I found I'd turned into a dog.
I looked at myself in the glass.
Same Ben with glasses and broken tooth stared back
But I just knew I was an alsatian.
'You're an alsatian,' I said to my reflection.
'Woof woof,' my reflection barked back.
No doubt about it, I was an alsatian.
I rushed into the bathroom
Where my sister was cleaning her teeth.
'I'm an alsatian,' I barked happily,
'My name's Attila.'
'Stop being stupid,' she said. 'I'm late for school.'
I sank my teeth into this piece of leg
That came out of a nightie.
'Good dog Attila,' she agreed.
I chased downstairs on all fours
Barking joyfully;
Being an alsatian called Attila agreed with me.
My new life came as a surprise to my mother
Since I have two sisters, a brother and a father
And not one of them is an alsatian.
'Good morning,' I barked to my mother and father
Giving a big grin and letting my tongue loll out.
'I'm an alsatian,' I said,
Standing on my back legs on the chair
And resting my paws in the All Bran.
'Stop dribbling and eat your breakfast properly,'
Said my mother.
'Woof woof,' I explained from my place under the sofa

Trying to eat a sausage without using my front paws.
'Your son's an alsatian,' said my mother.
'Dr McEever said we might see a sudden improvement,'
Said my father from behind his newspaper.
After the first shock, they soon got used to the idea
Of having a dog with spectacles called Attila
About the house;
Parents can be very adaptable
If you give them a chance.
It's a good life now,
A dog's life.
There's less homework, I don't have to shut doors
And I have my own place on a mat by the fire.
I spend my days sniffing and looking purposeful.
Some days I bury motor bikes
Or bits of sideboard in the cabbage patch.
Baby Sophie likes me a lot;
She gurgles and chuckles as I lick her face
Or try to herd the tortoise into her playpen
Suddenly I feel wanted.
My family speak to me a lot now
And are learning what my barks mean.
'Good boy Attila,' they say and tickle my ears.
My father spends hours taking me for walks
Or throwing sticks for me to bring back in my jaws.
And then to hear my mother calling
On some sunlit afternoon,
'Attila, Attila, time for cubs.'
And I romp up from the garden my tail wagging,
Weaving between the apple trees
And the white sheets on the line.
Well, there's nothing like it.
You really should try it sometime.

Arthur the Fat Boy

They said about Arthur
You're too fat
They said you can never win,
Only make a fool of yourself,
They said: Arthur think again.

But Arthur was sick of the insults
He was tired of all the names
He was fed up with never being asked to play
When they picked the teams for games.

So secretly he went running
In the evenings after tea
Past the allotments down to the old canal
Where he thought no one would see.

And there each night Arthur ran alone
Till his fat pink legs were numb
And the sweat on his face was a river
And his lungs beat like a drum.

He ran past locks and bridges
Where abandoned factories reared
Where the wind on the water called his name
And only the silence jeered.

Then finally sports day came around
And Arthur jogged to his place
And the mocking shouts of the jeering crowd
Made the tears course down his face.

But the jeers and the laughter died away
When the starter fired his gun
And a voice rang clear across the field:
Just look at that fat boy run.

Two laps from home and Arthur lies fourth
There's a map of pain on his face
And only his rage keeps him running
As he moves up into third place.

He inches up on the second boy
The leader's just ten yards ahead
And the voice of the crowd is a roar in his head
And the faces a sea of red.

And Arthur the fat boy sees the tape
And his pride has become a mine
And he scratches with his will for strength there
As his legs swim for the line.

And Arthur the fat boy makes first place
But the sky is upside down
And the finish appears to be moving away
As he falls to his knees on the ground.

He can hear the second boy closing fast
But his legs have turned to lead
And his brain can't hear his will power scream
Through the blizzard in his head.

And though for the first time in his life
He hears the crowd call his name
Arthur lies stranded high and alone
Beached on a rack of pain.

Then a mocking voice rings high and clear
It's a voice he's heard all his life
And the jeering, leering mockery
Twists in his heart like a knife.

And it's anger that sets him moving
Anger that lifts him again
It's anger that pushes his aching legs
Crawling across the line.

And Arthur the fat boy dreams he's in bed
And he clings to his dream in fear
So many cold mornings he's woken to see
His happiness disappear.

And Arthur reluctantly wakens himself
And the world turns like a wheel
And Arthur for the first time in his life
Awakes to a dream that's real.

Christmas Morning

On Christmas mornings
I wake up to see
What Father Christmas
Has brought for me.
Wrapped in my blanket
Like a cocoon
I wonder if this time
I've woken too soon.
Perhaps my stocking
Of blue and white
Will still be as empty
As it was last night.
Is it too early to take a peep?
But I'm too excited
To go back to sleep.
I crawl in the dark
To the foot of the bed
My heart bumping softly
With excitement and dread.
And yes! He's been,
There can be no doubt
The stocking's all bulges
When my hand reaches out.
When my family crowd shouting
In through my door
I know that Christmas
Has come round once more.

Sally won't you walk with me?

'Sally won't you walk with me
Walking heel and toe
Sally can we secrets share
As home from school we go?'

Arm in arm by lane and hedge
So many tales to tell
And every tale breeds tales anew
As we walk in a magic spell.

'And do you know what Brenda said
And how Alan banged his head
How Antonia cried at dinner time
And what Jemima said?'

'And wasn't dinner awful?
And Sally tell your dream
And will you come to tea next week?
And isn't Rose a scream?'

'Did you really tell your mother that
Did your sister cut your hair
Did you see that lady on the bike
Did you see those two boys stare?'

'And Sally look, stop giggling
Oh Sally honestly
Oh Sally don't you pull that face
Those people there will see.'

'What did your father say to that
And did you do it again?
You didn't really, I don't believe!
Sally what happened then?'

We whisper over Sally's gate
Till her mother calls her to tea
So many secrets still to tell
So many tales about me.

And if I could wish my days again
If time were a golden spool
I'd wish I could walk for ever
With Sally home from school.

Salcombe (1948)

Oh I remember how the sea
Came washing to our feet
That morning
And how my mother chanced to meet
Your mother
And father dozed in the August heat
And the gulls cried.

And how you said your name was Anne
And how my sister teased
Your cousin
And how your dog played as he pleased
In the waves
And barked and shook himself and sneezed
And the band played.

And how amongst the parasols and feet
We dug beneath the strand
A tunnel
And how my fingers wet with sand
Suddenly
Broke through and touched your stranger's hand
And the world turned.

The Pain

Coming home from school when I was seven
I told my mother of the pain.
'Where is the pain?' she asked.
'Here,' I said, holding before me
Two imaginary pillows in the air.
'Where were you when it started?'
'At Farnborough Road Juniors
But then I took it on the bus with me.'
'At what time did the pain start?'
'Between the end of dinner time
And the ringing of the bell for afternoon.'
'Was it something you ate? How did you notice it?'
'It walked through the door of Miss Mellor's class.
Before there was just me
Afterwards there were two of us,
The pain and me.'
'Was anything said? Did anybody notice?'
'Something was said about the register.
When the room was empty
The pain had made its home there.'
'Can't you tell me more?' my mother said.
She was getting bored with this conversation.
'What would you call the pain?'
'The pain is called Nancy Muriel Oliver
And is pale with yellow hair.
Is there nothing you can do,
Nothing you can say?'
'No,' said my mother,
Closing the medicine cabinet.
'Just go back to school tomorrow
And pray it never goes away.'

Invisible

It wasn't a sudden thing;
There were no falling stars
Or choirs of voices,
No rushes of wind
Or flashes of lightning –
I simply woke up one morning
And wasn't there.
Or at least,
I knew I was there
But there wasn't anything to be seen
That you might have called me.
If anybody had been there they would have seen
A huge smile of pride creasing my face,
That is if I had a face
For a smile to crease on.
It hadn't been easy;
Every day for nearly a year
I'd been trying to persuade my body
To have second thoughts
About being there.
In quiet corners unobserved
I'd order my body
To go away.
'Go away body,' I'd say
But my body seemed to need more convincing.
Down I'd look
And there it would still be,
Being there, all over the place.
I had a very stubborn body
Where being there was concerned.

But now all that effort
Seemed to be worthwhile.
I'm not saying I didn't have
Little doubts.
For example I said to myself,
'If you're not there anymore
Where are you?'
Or to put it another way,
How could I know
I wasn't there
If I wasn't there
To know that I wasn't.
After a bit
All this thinking
Started to make my head ache,
That is if I'd had a head
To make aches with.
I got up out of bed;
Put my clothes on my invisible body;
Washed my invisible face;
Brushed my invisible teeth
And took my invisible self on a walk
To meet the world.
It would be a day to remember
I promised myself.
What fun, I thought,
I'll have with my sister,
The postman,
The school librarian
And my haughty teacher with the spectacles
Miss Simpkins.
But
Although I told them

I was invisible
Nobody would believe
What they couldn't see
In front of their own eyes.
When the jug poured milk
As if by magic,
Instead of falling down
Into a faint with amazement
My sister said,
'You'll be late for school.'
The gate was pushed open
By an unseen hand;
But the postman only said,
'Two letters for you.'
Books flew unaided into the shelves;
'What a helpful boy,'
Said the librarian.
Spellings wrote themselves
Across my exercise book;
'Could do better,'
Wrote Miss Simpkins
In haughty red handwriting.
When I shouted at them all,
'I'm invisible,
I'm invisible,
Look at me, I'm invisible!'
They all smiled
The same tight-lipped smile.
They don't know
That they can't see me.

Christmas at our House

The Christmases at our house
Aren't like the pictures I've seen
On calendars and Christmas cards
Where all is joy serene,
Where red-faced husbands kiss their wives
Beneath sprigs of mistletoe
And fat little angels sing carols
And it always seems to snow.
For a start my Dad starts moaning
Before he's even out of bed
And Elvis, my brother, starts screaming
When his Action Man loses his head.
And Ann won't touch her turkey
And Elvis starts calling her names
And Dad overdoes the brandy
And the pudding bursts into flames.
Auntie May starts singing long, sad hymns
And the mongrel is sick on the mat
While Uncle George gets merry
On just three glasses of sherry
And spills custard all over the cat.
After tea we play disorganized games
And Gran faints away in her chair
And the games always end in tears and sulks
Because Elvis will never play fair.
Sharron falls out with her boyfriend,
Tina stops talking to hers,
Then we have to call the fire brigade
When Tom's head gets stuck in the stairs.

I breathe a sigh of relief when midnight arrives
And the relations all disappear
Because I know for certain that Christmas Day
Won't be round for another whole year.

Growing up

I know a lad called Billy
Who goes along with me
He plays this game
Where he uses my name
And makes people think that he's me.

Don't ever mess with Billy
He's a vicious sort of bloke
He'll give you a clout
For saying nowt
And thump you for a joke.

My family can't stand Billy
Can't bear him round the place
He won't eat his food
He's rough and he's rude
And wears scowls all over his face.

No one can ever break Billy
He's got this look in his eye
That seems to say
You can wale me all day
But you'll not make Billy cry.

He has a crazy face has Billy
Eyes that look but can't see
A mouth like a latch
Ears that don't match
And a space where his brain should be.

Mad Billy left one morning
Crept away without being seen
Left his body for me
That fits perfectly
And a calm where his madness had been.

Mandy likes the Mud

Polly likes to play with toys
Melissa makes a lot of noise
Ann has a bike
Trevor a trike
But Mandy likes the mud.
She jumps in it
She slumps in it
She scoops it in her hands
She rides on it
She slides on it
She digs to foreign lands.

Kevan likes to kick a ball
Peter never plays at all
Tina cooks tarts
Donna plays darts
But Mandy loves the mud.
She galumphs in it
She splarges
She glugs and slurps and slops
She grins in it
She swims in it
She does smacking belly flops.

Tricia talks to her teddy bear
Belinda combs her doll's long hair
Tracy plays tennis
Mark is a menace
But Mandy adores the mud.

She dives in it
She thrives in it
She paints it on the wall
She goes splash in it
She goes splosh in it
She does the breast stroke and the crawl.

Ronnie likes falling
And snowballing in snow
Lucy is learning how to row
Louise loves a sing-song
Paula likes ping-pong
But Mandy rejoices in mud.
She has sat in it
Filled her hat with it
She washed the neighbour's cat in it
She hid from Mum in it
Banged her drum in it
She fell down on her bum in it.

Kenneth kicks an old tin can
Anthony plays with his Action Man
Wanda is waiting
For Sam to go skating
But Mandy lives in the mud.
So if you're looking for Mandy
Find the muddiest mess
At Mud House, Mud Corner
Her permanent muddress.

The Building Site

In a haze of brick dust
And red sun
All day long the men slog,
Lumbering about
The churned ridges of clay
In clod-hopping boots,
Humping great hods
On the brawn of red shoulders
Up piped and rattling scaffolds
And uneven boards
To where their mates
With deft flicks from trowels
Make house walls grow
Brick by red brick.
All day too
The great trucks bang and clatter
Back and forth
And the churning mixer
Slops out gobs of concrete
In wholesome pats
Onto the dusty earth.

At twelve
They break off
And swarm from scaffolding
To drink brown tea
From huge mugs
That they grip in the beef of their fists.
After, they kick a ball about
Or lie and bronzy in the sun
Until it's turn-to time again.

The afternoon shift wears on;
They whistle more,
Shout and laugh
And sing the songs
That blare from two transistors.
At six they knock off
And pack into a lorry
With their clobber.
Down the rutted track they bound
Shouting and cheering.
When the pandemonium clears,
The shells of houses stand
Workmanless, untenanted and still.
Silence in the settling haze.
A sparrow bounces on rubble,
A curious mongrel snuffles
On a tail-wagging inspection tour,
Finds it good
And departs for an important meeting.
I wouldn't mind being a labourer
For a bit.

The Vandalingo

In the rotting lake called Albion
That's thick as kedgeree
Lurks the odious Vandalingo
With his scurvy wife Debris.

Beneath a rusting gas fire
Near an old bike and a plank
The Vandalingo makes his home
In a waste disposal tank.

His carcass smells of wellingtons
His boots are size fifteen
His nails leak inky messages
To his baby son Globscene.

His teeth are broken hacksaw blades
His lips drip kerosene
He belches fumes and poison gas
From his lungs of polythene.

For years he sleeps his dreamless sleeps
Amongst rusting beds and cars
But then one night he rises up
To sport beneath the stars.

And then through webs of rotting weeds
Two spinning fog lamps loom
As the Vandalingo's yellow eyes
Peer dimly through the gloom.

The surface of the rotting lake
Lifts like a tent of slime
As the Vandalingo crashes through
To chant his ancient rhyme.

'Tonight I vandalinger
And though I'm rarely seen
From the broken trail I leave behind
You'll know where I have been.

'I crash through walls and hedges
I uproot flowers and trees
I spread garbage, swill and bacon rind
Where they're sure to cause disease.

'I scrawl my name on subway walls
I chew the seats on trains
I hurl prams and bottles into ponds
And my head through window panes.'

And if your school's been flooded
And there's ink down every wall
You'll know that sometime in the night
The Vandalingo's called.

As dawn creeps up the city streets
He drags home 'neath the moon's pale stare
And in a belch of bubbling mud
Sinks gurgling to his lair.

And there he's joyfully welcomed
By Globscene and his spouse Debris
And to the waking world above
They wail this song of glee.

'We are the Vandalingos
There's but one thought in our brain
That though we sleep ten thousand years
Our time will come again.'

The Old Man of Wells

Here sit I
Glum and alone
Stuck on my column
Of freezing stone,
Here crouch I
The Old Man of Wells
Battered and deafened
By the clatter of bells.
Eternal eyes
Gazing South
Eternal finger
In eternal mouth.
Rubbing my tooth
In rain and sleet
While uncaring centuries
Crawl 'neath my feet.
Saint Appolina
To you I pray
Make a miracle take
My pain away.
But she has no pity
On my pain
Only the West Wind
Hears me complain.
Why put *me* here
In this holy place
With my wine-jug ears
And gormless face.
Raised in a byre
With two pigs and a hen
Now my neighbours are holy men.

'There's your gargoyle,'
I heard the Abbot shout,
'Stick a pipe in his mouth
For the rain to spill out.'
The poor can't argue
With the likes of he,
If he wants a gargoyle
That's what I'll be.
So kind mortals
Who stand and stare
Consider my tooth
When you kneel in prayer.
Pray that this wound
In my tooth may mend
And that like this poem
The pain will end.

On a pillar in Wells Cathedral is the effigy of a peasant who suffers agonies of toothache and rubs the bad tooth with his finger.

Saint Appolina is the patron saint of those who suffer from the toothache.

A gargoyle is a figure, usually grotesque, either man or animal or a mixture of both who has a spout in his mouth in order to carry rain water clear of the Cathedral wall.

Wedding Day

Lillian McEever is bride for the day
Wearing Mummy's old wedding dress long locked away
And a posy of dandelions for her bouquet
And a tiara of daisies.

Birdsong showers silver on Institute Drive
Where Lillian waits for her guests to arrive
And the shouts and the laughter shake the morning alive
There's a wedding today.

Past the brook they wind where the cherry trees bloom
Casting white showers of blossom over bride and groom
And grandmothers dream in curtained front rooms
And remember.

Lillian McEever forget not this day
For Spring mornings die but memories stay
When the past like the dress is long locked away
And the leaves fall.

Skipping Song

Ann and Belinda
Turning the rope
Helen jumps in
But she hasn't got a hope
Helen Freckles
What will you do
Skip on the table
In the Irish stew
Freckles on her face
Freckles on her nose
Freckles on her bum
Freckles on her toes
Helen Freckles
Tell me true
How many freckles
Have you got on you
One two three four five six seven
And out goes you.

Stella Starwars
Skip in soon
Into your spaceship
And off to the moon
Skip on the pavement
One and two
Skip like a rabbit
Or a kangaroo
Skip so high
You never come down

Over the steeples
Over the town
Skip over rooftops
Skip over trees
Skip over rivers
Skip over seas
Skip over London
Skip over Rome
Skip all night
And never come home
Skip over moonbeams
Skip over Mars
Skip through the Milky Way
And try to count the stars
One two three four five six seven
Out goes you.

Space Shot

Out of the furnace
The great fish rose
Its silver tail on fire
But with a slowness
Like something sorry
To be rid of earth.
The boiling mountains
Of snow white cloud
Searched for a space to go into
And the ground thundered
With a roar
That set teacups
Rattling in a kitchen
Twenty miles away.
Across the blue it arched
Milk bottle white
But shimmering in the haze.
And the watchers by the fence
Held tinted glass against their eyes
And wondered at what man could do
To make so large a thing
To fly so far and free.
While the unknown Universe waited;
For waiting
Was what it had always been good at.

Moonscape 2400

With each dawning
The older colonists
Who had arrived in the first ships
During the Summer 2320
Settle themselves
Into the Viewing Quadrant
To watch the Earth rise
Like a blackened marble.
Their eyes expressionless,
They make a picture of
How it was creep into their minds.
Master Control cannot see this
And anyway the men
Are too old to be dangerous.
The third generation
Call out each other's numbers
And crowd about the flashing boxes
In the Electro Pleasure Dome.
In the dust beyond the city
Coca-Cola tins fill the craters
And one boy is slapped
For asking what memory is.

Lessons in History

After three orbits
Of the unknown planet
The multi-spectral scanner
Showed vegetation
But no other life.
When we told Command
That we were going in,
We felt their excitement
Through the stream of data;
The benefits of colonization
Were apparent to us all.
They left the descent decision to us
And wished us every kind of luck.
The logic bank was reassuring:
— REMEMBER ALWAYS YOU ARE MEN.
— HISTORY HAS ALWAYS PROVED
THE SUPERIORITY OF EXPLORERS.
— THEY MUST BE YOUR INFERIORS
OR THEY WOULD HAVE FOUND YOU FIRST.
We powered the retros and descended.
The jungle smothered us
In heat and darkness
But to the east a bloom of light
And in the light a rumbling
That one of us remarked
Was like a voice.
Moving forward
The light became a square
And the voice clearer.

We thought of the logic bank
And advanced, our weapons ready.
Somehow the square of light grew smaller
And we filled it with our heads.
The four of us peered out
Into something like a hall
With many people watching us.
We heard the historian say,
'And so two thousand years ago
Our forefathers arrived,'
Before his hand moved
Towards the off switch.

Message Understood

The Scantext stutters
'ALERT' in my brain.
I await further instructions.
The message comes through.
'SOLUTION CONCERNING THE ROBOTS.'
This has been expected.
I await further instructions.
My personal robot tries to read
The message in my brain
But my hypocrisy defeats him.
He smiles back at my false smile.
In many ways he is almost human.
The message is absorbed.
'THE ROBOTS HAVE OUTLIVED THEIR USE.
THEIR AMBITION THREATENS US.'
I await further instructions.
'LAST WEEK THREE OF THEM
WERE SEEN DANCING AND SINGING
IN THE DESERTED BALLROOM.'
I await further instructions.
'IF EACH HUMAN PLAYS HIS PART
THEN NO ONE WILL BE GUILTY.'
Message understood.
I prime my hand laser.
My robot turns to me
With something in his face
That in a man you might call fear.
For three seconds I squeeze the trigger.
The fine rod of light penetrates him.

He falls to the ground
His eyes turning to water.
Something like a song
Invades his throat
And his mouth leaks red.
Soon the threat will be over
If all humans do their duty.
Humming to myself
I await further instructions.

Shed in Space

My Grandad Lewis
On my mother's side
Had two ambitions.
One was to take first prize
For shallots at the village show
And the second
Was to be a space commander.
Every Tuesday
After I'd got their messages,
He'd lead me with a wink
To his garden shed
And there, amongst the linseed
And the sacks of peat and horse manure
He'd light his pipe
And settle in his deck chair.
His old eyes on the blue and distant
That no one else could see,
He'd ask,
'Are we A-OK for lift off?'
Gripping the handles of the lawn mower
I'd reply:
'A-OK.'
And then
Facing the workbench,
In front of shelves of paint and creosote
And racks of glistening chisels
He'd talk to Mission Control.
'Five-Four-Three-Two-One-Zero –
We have lift off.
This is Grandad Lewis talking,

Do you read me?
Britain's first space shed
Is rising majestically into orbit
From its launch pad
In the allotments
In Lakey Lane.'

And so we'd fly,
Through timeless afternoons
Till tea time came,
Amongst the planets
And mysterious suns,
While the world
Receded like a dream:
Grandad never won
That prize for shallots,
But as the captain
Of an intergalactic shed
There was no one to touch him.

Johnny come over the pasture

Johnny come over the pasture
Where the corn waves like the sea
Johnny come race me to the moon
Before we go home for tea.

Climb up here beside me
We'll ride on the old farm gate
We must reach the moon by five o'clock
Or else we'll be too late.

There's banana sandwiches and beans
And salmon paste and spam
And three sorts of jelly to fill your belly
And cake with marzipan.

Johnny the moon grows larger
But mother's calling me
Let's leave the moon until later
After we've both had tea.

Magdalena

By Lakey Lane allotments
Past the stream near Batty's Farm
Past the Laundry I go running
With Magdalena 'neath my arm.

Magdalena is a wonder
Her sails gleam purest white,
Her hull's the hue of a skylark's egg
She moves like an eagle's flight.

Magdalena on the water
Magdalena ship serene
Magdalena riding on the wind
Like a schooner in a dream.

And on certain Summer mornings
When no one else's near
I lay my head upon the grass
And through half-closed eyes I peer

At Magdalena gliding
And her wake is like a sigh
And her sails tower white and billowing
Against the arched blue of the sky.

And the soft breeze on the water
Brings to me gently winging
The creak of a ghostly windlass
And long dead voices singing.

Six Views of a Waterfall

When the river threw itself off the cliff
It spun a twist of rope
So as not to lose touch with itself.

The river of a sudden
Tired of lying down between fields
And having the sky painted on its face
Stood up and was pleased.

Around the holy water where the miracle happened
They hollowed out a damp chapel
And glued green carpets on the wall to absorb the sound.
Every day someone brings fresh ferns.

We can see the silent film through the beaded curtain
There is interference on the vertical hold
And for a comedy there should be subtitles,
But the actors shout just the same.

Sometimes the river stays still
And children swim upstream.
After a time they lie down and walk away.

At home they have sardines for tea
And later go to bed.
While this is going on
The waterfall does what it has always done
And doesn't dream about people.

Song of the City

My brain is stiff with concrete
My limbs are rods of steel
My belly's stuffed with money
My soul was bought in a deal.

They poured metal through my arteries
They choked my lungs with lead
They churned my blood to plastic
They put murder into my head.

I'd a face like a map of the weather
Flesh that grew to the bone
But they tore my story out of my eyes
And turned my heart to stone.

Let me wind from my source like a river
Let me grow like wheat from the grain
Let me hold out my arms like a natural tree
Let my children love me again.

My Granny is a Sumo Wrestler

My Granny is a Sumo Wrestler

My granny is six foot three
My granny is built like a tree
My granny says – *Nothing*
I mean nothing
Frightens me.

When Granny walks down the streets
She scares every man she meets
Nobody gonna mess with her
My granny is a Sumo Wrestler.

My granny is six foot three
My granny she's built like a tree
My granny says – *Nothing*
I mean nothing
Frightens me.

My granny does what she likes
My granny rides two motor bikes (at the same time)
My granny she breaks down doors
My granny bends bars with her jaws.

My granny she's six foot three (that's sitting down)
My granny she's built like a tree
My granny says – *Nothing*
Absolutely nothing
Frightens me.

My granny is a railway ganger
My granny is a wild head banger
My granny eats uncooked bison
My granny beat up Mike Tyson (in the first round).

My granny she's six foot three
My granny she's built like a tree (oak tree)
My granny says – *Nothing*
And I mean nothing
Ever
    Ever
        EVER
           Frightens me.

The Artist

I painted a brilliant picture
The greatest ever seen
It hung in the National Gallery
And was purchased by the Queen.
This most wonderful of paintings
Is called 'Polar Bears in the Snow'
And in case you don't believe me
I've included it below.

New Boy

He stood alone in the playground
Scuffed his shoes and stared at the ground
He'd come halfway through term from the Catholic school
On the other side of town.

He'd a brand new blazer and cap on
Polished shoes and neatly cut hair
Blew on his fists, looked up and half-smiled
Pretending he didn't care.

And I remembered when I'd been new
And no one had spoken to me
I'd almost cried as I stood alone
Hiding my misery.

Heart said I should go over,
Share a joke or play the fool
But I was scared of looking stupid
In front of the rest of the school.

At break someone said they'd seen him
Crying in the geography test
And when he came out they pointed and laughed
And I laughed along with the rest.

In my dreams I'd always stood alone
Believing I was the best
But in the cold playground of everyday life
I was no better than the rest.

Genes

They say I've got my father's nose
They say I've got his walk
And there's something about my grandad
In the serious way I talk.

'And aren't his legs just like our Jack's?'
Says smiling Auntie Rose
'*He* could bend over just like that
And touch his head with his toes.'

I've got Auntie Julia's funny laugh
I've sister Betty's lips
And just like Sid on my mother's side
I'm fond of fish and chips.

I have moods that remind them of Auntie Vi
And my hair's just like their Paul
When I look at myself in the mirror at home
I wonder if I'm me at all.

But what I ask myself is this –
Why does it have to be
Me who looks like them and not
Them who look like me?

Empty House

I hate our house when there's no one in
I miss my family and I miss the din.
The rooms and the hallway seem cold and bare
And the silence hangs like dust in the air.
What's that sound upstairs that makes me start
Driving Fear like an icicle through my heart?
I'm imagining things, there's nobody there –
But I have to make sure so I creep up the stair.
I stand holding my breath by the bedroom door
And hear something rustling across the floor.
Then a scratching sound, a tiny cry!
I can't seem to breathe, my throat is dry.
In the silence I hear my own heart beating
And the rumble of water in the central heating.
I should go in but I just don't dare
So I call aloud, 'Is anyone there?'
Nobody answers. I push open the door
A fluttering shadow crosses the floor.
And now I see him, now understand
And I gather him gently in my hands.
'I won't hurt you, my friend. Don't flutter, don't start.'
But his body beats wild like a feathered heart.
Out through the window, watch him wheel and fly
Carrying my fear across the sky.

The Boyhood of Dracula

So we let him join us
In the game of Hide and Seek
Because Joanna said we ought,
She being the biggest of us all
And bossy with it.
And him standing there
All hunched and trembling
In the thin snow by the stable door
Watching us like some poor lost soul
With those great eyes he had.
Well, you'd be a thing of stone
To take no pity on the boy.
You never saw a soul
So pale and woebegone;
His pinched nose raw with cold
And naught to keep the bitter wind
The right side of his bones
But that old bit of musty cloak
He always seems to wear.

Poor little mite
You'd think, to watch,
He'd never played the game before.
Maureen Cantelow,
The parson's youngest girl
From Norton Campion way,
She found him straight away
Hardly bothering to hide at all
Among the meal sacks
In the lower barn.

Poor girl,
She must have cut herself
In there somehow
For as I spied them
Running hand in hand below
She sowed fresh seeds of crimson blood
Across ridged and bitter snow.

Moon

'The moon is thousands of miles away,'
My Uncle Trevor said.
Why can't he see
It's caught in a tree
Above our onion bed?

Talking to Trees

Grandad talks to trees
When the garden's empty.
'Hello, Oak,' he says,
'How do, Willow?
How's tricks this morning, Ash?'
Then he moves on down
To the fruit and veg
Like a general
Inspecting a line of troops.
'Well now, Rhubarb,
You've come on a bundle
Since I saw you last.
How's my old mate Sprout?'

Mum was embarrassed
In case the neighbours heard.
And Dad asked
Laughing up his sleeve,
'Don't they ever answer back?'
''Course they don't,'
Said Grandad.
'That's the whole point.
What d'you think they are?
People?'

Death of a Ghost

Now none of us had ever
Actually seen the ghost,
Though some – like Raymond Pudsey
And his mate – would boast
They'd once stayed out all night
And seen it striding
At midnight past the ditch
Where they were hiding.
'Course, none of us believed
A word of it. *I* knew –
We *all* knew – Raymond Pudsey
Never spoke a true
Word in his life. But then
All of us believed the tales
Of the ghostly knight who
Roamed the hills and dales
Searching for the bitter foe
Who'd stabbed him one dark night
Nine hundred years ago.

They said the wounds from which
The knight had died
Still dripped fresh blood
That never, ever dried.
Many's the night I lay
In bed and couldn't sleep
Imagining I heard his footsteps
Climbing up the steep,
Rough pathway to our house.
My grandma'd threaten me

If I should misbehave with,
'Sure as sure one day
He'll rise up from the grave
And carry you away.'
'Don't you believe a word
She says,' my dad would say.
But even now sometimes
I wake up in the night
And think he's out there waiting,
Somewhere beyond the light.

Did anybody see it?
Colley's grandad did,
When rolling home one night
From Weston Dale so dead
With drink he slipped and fell
Into a field of corn –
This was long before
You or me was born.
He clambered to his feet again
And stumbled swearing
Through this sea of grain
The thorns and brambles tearing
At his clothes until
He staggered down the Fosse
Out on the moorland
Where the four lanes cross.
He stops. Hears a sound
And turning, sees this shadow
Rising from the ground.
'Course, first of all he thinks
What anyone would think:
Here's another bound for home

Something the worse for drink.
So Colley's grandad cries aloud,
'Who's there? Give me your aid!'
And not a word the stranger says
But three times waves a shimmering blade
Above his head, and striding past
Seems to vanish into air
Leaving the sound of battle
Still raging everywhere.

What was it like?
Its face was pale. It wore
A sort of chain mail hood
Which Colley's grandad swore
Was dyed deep red with rust
Or maybe it was blood.
Its eyes were closed,
The mouth a gaping wound
Screaming for revenge
But yet it made no sound.
As it passed it seemed
To do its best to strike
At Colley's grandad with
A kind of lance or pike.
And that was all.

Old Colley ran,
His feet scarce touched the ground
Until he shut the door
Behind him, safe and sound.
Shaking with fright, he fell
Into his bed and wept

With fear at what he'd seen
Till finally he slept.

The sun shone bright, the birds
Sang sweet the following day.
The apparition seemed
A million miles away.
Old Colley laughed and told his wife
What drink had made him see,
But she turned pale as gin
And pointed fearfully
To where her husband stood.

The white shirt that he wore
Ran red with crimson blood.
No matter how they tried
The blood flowed swift and fresh
Although no wound nor mark
Had scarred his flesh.

Well, that's our village legend
I've nothing more to say –
Except for something strange
That happened just the other day.
An Oxford archaeologist
Began to dig the ground
Where folk there reckoned
The knight would likeliest be found.
For three long weeks he dug
While we all watched, our faces grim
Whispering to each other,
'What has *our* ghost to do with him?'

Then, one cold morning
Six feet beneath the ground
The man unearthed a coffin
And inside it found
Remains. The whole village
Stared in deep dismay
As our poor ghost was dragged into
The clear light of day;
A tiny pile of mouldering bones,
Broken wood and rust
And in the steady falling rain
A legend slowly turning into dust.

Why Did You Call Me Percy?

Dad, why did you call me Percy?
Why did you give me that name?
I only have to think of it
And I go puce with shame.
Mum, why did you call me Percy?
It's a name that no one would want
Did you suffer some kind of brainstorm
When you named me at the font?
What was wrong with David
Or Fred or Wayne or Sam
Or any other kind of name
That sounds like what I am?
Percy sounds like someone
Who helps his mother cook
Brings apples for the teacher
Presses wild flowers in a book.
Who goes skipping through the countryside
Or keeps a budgie for a pet
Who cries when soap gets in his eyes
Or when his feet get wet.

I'd love to be something like Conan
Or someone with a name like Keith
Who sings and dances on the stage
And plays guitars with his teeth.
And what was wrong with Eddie
Or Rod or Cliff or Rick
Or Jimmy, Ben or Phil or Geoff
Or Elvis, John or Mick?
But Percy, stupid Percy
It goes through me like a knife
Did you never think when you called me that
He'd be with me all my life?

Mazurkatee

Mazurkatee the brindled cat
Leapt smiling from the ark
And hitched a lift to Humansville
Where he thought he'd have a lark.
He jumped aboard a pick-up truck
That drove him into town
And flashed his smile at all he met
While sauntering up and down.
The lady at the check-out till
Was straightening up her seams
Applying rouge to both her cheeks
And adding up her dreams.

Beneath the portals of the bank
A rich man knelt and prayed
To a statue dedicated
To the money he had made.
And on the ancient shores of Time
A ragged beggar sat
His pockets full of emptiness
And raindrops in his hat.
And the cat they called Mazurkatee
Could read the hearts of men
And all that he found written there
He multiplied by ten.
And when he'd learned what all men know
He stored it in his brain
Then sat forever in a tree
And never smiled again.

Ambitions

'When you grow up what will you be?'
I opened my dictionary at random to see
And stabbed with my finger,
'That's what I'll be.
Has anyone heard of lycanthropy?'

My Bed's a Silver Spaceship

When I wake up some mornings
Not all is what it seems
I drift in a land of make-believe
Between my real life and my dreams.

Strange creatures from the stories
That I read the night before
Crowd in upon my drowsiness
Through imagination's door.

Where sleep and waking overlap
The alarm clock's jangling cry
Is a roaring fire-tailed rocket
Hurtling through the sky.

My bed's a silver spaceship
Which I pilot all alone
Whispering through endless stratospheres
Towards planets still unknown.

Outside through morning mistiness
The spinning lights of cars
In my make-believe space voyage
Become eternities of stars.

Is that mother calling something
My dreams can't understand?
Or can it be crackling instructions
From far-off Mission Command?

If I make believe my ceiling
Is space through which I fly
If I make believe my bedroom
Is my capsule flying high
If I make believe the light bulb
Is a planet passing by
If I make believe my blanket
Is its cratered surface dry
Then that's what it is for me
Yes, that's what it is
That's what it is
That's what it is for me.

Universal Zoo

The creatures of the world one day
Packed sandwiches and tea
And toured the Universal Zoo
To see what they could see.

And all alone in a tiny cage
Sat a child on an unmade bed
With the words 'Endangered Species' scrawled
On the wall above his head.

Today We're Going to Write a Poem!

I close my eyes and try to drift
Into a world of poetry thoughts.
You know the kind of thing they like:
Clouds and snow and nodding daffodils.
But then I see my Uncle Glynn at Grendon Green
Whistling in his herd of cows.
They trundle through the muck into the shed
Their heavy udders swaying
Veined, and full of milk.
Then suddenly my mum is there
Selling these moccasins
That she makes at home
To sell at Ledbury Market.
The paper bag is twirled till it has ears.
She flings a shower of coins into the till.
I shake my head. This won't do.
You can't write poems about moccasins
Udders, money, muck and tills.
I push my mind back to poetic thoughts:
Clouds, banks of snow and dancing daffodils.

Paper Wrap

This is me on a roll
At the back of a shop
Only wrapping paper
But I'm full of hip-hop.

Wanna wrap a kettle
Wanna wrap a china cup
Tear me off a stripperoo
And watch me wrap them up.

Cos I'm wrapping paper
Wrap anything you see
But no one gives a monkey's
When they're all through with me.

They take me to their houses
And, isn't this a sin?
They rip me all to pieces
And chuck me in a bin.

And me, I'm getting tired
I'm a roll of misery
Dream of breaking out of here
Dream of being free.

So one rainy evening
When I'd really had enough
Made my mind up there and then
I was going to cut up rough.

Waited in the darkness
Until they closed the shop
Then started to unroll myself
I just wouldn't stop.

Heard the watchman singing
His finger on his gun
Jumped him down by Fancy Goods
His singing days were done.

He didn't know what hit him
Didn't even shout
When wrapping paper's on the loose
You'd better all look out.

I snaked across the counter
And stole across the floor
Heard the city calling me
And smashed out through the door.

The patrolman shone his flashlight
Radioed back to base
'There's something weird near Harrods
And it doesn't have a face!'

The policeman gasped with terror
'Is this a joke?' he muttered
They were the final words, my friends
That flatfoot ever uttered.

A cleaner in the sewer
Working far below
No one heard his dying cry,
'It's the Wrapper! **No!** Oh *Noooooooooooooo!*'

Rolling through the midnight streets
Wrap anyone I see
Schoolgirls, priests or criminals
All come the same to me.

There's a pair of late-night lovers
Five revellers in the rain
A drunken man who'll never see
His home, sweet home, again.

And it's – Look out! Here's the bogeyman
Better close your doors
The next house that I visit
Could be yours or yours or yours.

If you peep out through your curtains
That's my shadow on the sky
So hide your eyes my darlings
When the Wrapper's rolling by.

And little children everywhere
Don't ask your mummies why
Just close your eyes my darlings
When I come rolling by.

And it's – **NIGHTMARE ON WRAP STREET!**
It's headlines in the paper
It's – **ENTIRE CITY EATEN ALIVE
    BY PSYCHO WRAPPING PAPER.**

The minister chews his fingernails
There are questions in the press
Vera Lynn is singing songs
To the troops and the SAS.

It's – **'Batman, do you read me?**
    Please save us if you can.'
It's – **'Call the good ship Enterprise'**
It's – **'Send for Superman.'**

But me, I'm right behind you
As the night begins to lift
Wrapping up the BBC
Like a pretty Christmas gift.

10 Downing Street and Oxford Street
St Paul's, The Albert Hall,
Just throw myself around them
Wrap one, wrap two, wrap all.

Wrapped up Heathrow Airport
And Concorde flying over
Wrapped up tight the Sussex Downs
And the white cliffs of Dover.

Rolled myself down Wembley Way
Wrapped up all the players
Rolled across to Kathmandu
There go the Himalayas.

And now the round and turning world
Was gift-wrapped tight and neat
There was nothing left for me to do
My life's work was complete.

Felt a touch of emptiness
Turned back to my old shelf
There was nothing left to wrap around
So I wrapped around . . .

Midnight Snow

Taken from the Welsh hymn:
Y Milwr Bychan by Joseph Parry

One night as I lay sleeping
And dreams ran through my head
The night breeze stirred my curtain
And moonlight bathed my bed.
I walked up to the window
And leaned upon the ledge
Saw drifting snowflakes falling
On road and lane and hedge.

Midnight snow
Drifting slow
While the world lies sleeping
And only me, here to see
Those snowflakes gently falling.

And all along the roadway
The blanket lies unstirred
No tracks of tyres or sledges
No print of fox or bird.
No footsteps in the garden
No sound upon the air
A million petals falling
Silent as a prayer.

Midnight snow
Drifting slow
While the world lies sleeping
And only me, here to see
Those snowflakes gently falling.

The Human Exhibition

In the Museum of Mankind
Mum gave me this look
When I said so loud
That everyone could hear,
      'I want to go to the toilet.'
Dad looked at his watch.
'We'll meet you by Human Growth
In five minutes from now.'
As I walked away I heard
Uncle Peter say to Auntie Lill,
'Let's visit the dinosaurs
And meet some of your relations.'

When I came out
I couldn't see them anywhere
And ran into a room called
Life Before Birth.
All of a sudden the lights went out
And a robot voice whispered,
      'This is your mother!'
A gigantic ten foot baby
Lit from inside
Hung pink and hovering in the air
Its heartbeat thundering out.
It was a relief to see Dad's bald head at last
Gleaming beneath a Human Ageing sign.

But when I tapped him on the back
He had the wrong face on.
     'Sorry, sorry,' I said
And ran towards the entrance
Searching the faces
For someone that I knew
But all the world was strangers.
Lost, I thought. I'm lost
And though I didn't want them to
Hot tears came in my eyes.
I ran back to Life Before Birth
But my mum was nowhere.

An old lady in a floor-length kilt
Offered me her lacy hanky
To wipe away my tears
Then passed me on to this attendant.
He led me through
Lost Tribes of the Amazon Rainforest.
     'Anyone here you know?' he asked.
I shook my head.
When a boy with green hair
And a skull and crossbones on his jacket
     Said, *'Look, that kid's crying!'*
I pretended I had something in my eye.

Then looking round I saw my Uncle Peter
Pretending he was playing the xylophone
On the pterodactyl's tail
And Auntie Lill crimson round the neck
Pretending she was on her own.
Mum squealed and hugged me till I squeaked
Then told me off for half an hour
Then cried and hugged me once again.

We went to the café for tea
And Uncle Peter bought me
An Angelica doughnut with cherries on the top.
I looked round.
All those people!
Feeding their faces fit to bust,
Slurping tea and fizzy drinks
Cheeks munching and bulging
Bulging and munching.
The Human Exhibition.

Nightmare

Someone came walking through my dreams
Across a lake of blood
And though I turned to run, my feet
Were rooted where they stood.

Within the prison of my dream
I struggled to break free
But nearer and nearer the figure came
Across the lake to me.

The hollow sockets of his eyes
Held me in his glare
And though I raised my voice to scream
My voice was soundless air.

At last I woke but still my heart
Beat with an awful dread
For there the sightless figure stood
Smiling beside my bed.

In a Pickle

Antoinette Pickles
Never moved far
Lived with pickled onions
In a pickled-onion jar.
Onions on her right side
Onions on the other
Onions at her head and heels
All bottled by her mother.

Her friends who came to visit her
Were all distinctly tickled
To read the label on the jar,
'Here's Antoinette, quite pickled.'

The Midnight Mail

Have you ever woken up
In the middle of the night?
Have you ever woken up
In an awful fright?

Have you woken from a dream
With a dreadful start?
And heard a drum beating
A tattoo in your heart?

And the night is as black
As a witch's hat
And you think to yourself
What was that? What was that?

What was that? What was that?
Made the windows shake
Made the saucepans rattle
And the whole house quake?

What was that? What was that?
It's the Midnight Mail
Thundering past my bedroom.
On its iron rail.

Now further off and further off,
Out of earshot, out of sight
Swifter than an arrow
Hurtling through the night.

Now quieter and more quiet
Till a still silence falls
On trees and roads and houses
And moss-covered walls.

And I think about the Midnight Mail
Thundering on her way
Waking someone in a bedroom
A hundred miles away.

Kite

On Parbold Hill my red kite swirled
Caught in the same high draught that whirled
The crows and set the grey torn shreds
Of cloudlets streaming overhead.
It tugged my fist insistently
Like something longing to be free
Of earth. And oh, I dreamed we two
Soared on the air as wild birds do
Breasting the west wind, ever higher
Over the fields of Lancashire
Out of the clouds, into the light
Smaller now and gaining height
Until at long last out of sight.

Life as a Sheep

Sometimes
Oi stands
Sometimes
Oi sits
Then
Stands again
Then
Sits
For a bit.

Sometimes
Oi wanders
Sometimes
Oi stays
Sometimes
Oi chews
Sometimes
Oi strays.

Sometimes
Oi coughs
Sometimes
Oi don't
Sometimes
Oi bleats
Sometimes
Oi won't.

Sometimes
Oi watch
The human race
Or
Smiles to meself
Or
Stares into space.

And when
Oi's happy
Oi'd dance and sing
But Oi
Don't have the knack
To do
Such a thing.

At night
Oi lays
By the old church steeple
And
Falls asleep
By counting people.

Funny Man

There's a funny bloke called Albert
Lives at Number Twenty-Five
Plays a silver cornet with his ear
Keeps piglets in a hive.

He dances on his ownsome
By the lightsome brightsome stars
And keeps giant snails in metal pails
And his teeth in pickle jars.

He bathes starkers in a barrel
Beneath a hornbeam tree
And hides his head inside a sack
In case anyone should see.

He mows his bathroom carpet
And hoovers all the grass
Sings cadenzas to the sparrows
As they flitter-flutter past.

Wears a suit of rusty armour
Whenever he's in bed
And a green and yellow cosy
To warm his old, bald head.

But you'd best not laugh at Albert
You'd best not mock, my dears
For Albert could be you, d'you see
In sixty-five short years.

Reflections

Here we are
At the mirror
Again
Me and him
Him and me
Staring and changing
Changing and staring.
Every single day
It's like this;
That hair
Those eyes
That nose.
And he
That other one there
Know what he does?
Gives me that smile
That sincere smile
The one he tries on me each day.
And me? I smile straight back.
He doesn't fool me
Not for a minute
That smile may work on others
Not on me.
I tell him straight
No messing.
I say – 'Listen you,
Whoever you are,
I can see through you
See through that smile.
You want to be careful.

I know what you're about
Better watch your step
Or with a tiny breath
I'll wipe you out.'

Cousin Janice with the Big Voice

When my cousin Janice
Opens her mouth to speak
A storm kindles behind her teeth
And a gale pours out.
This is a voice used
To holding conversations
With cows and sheep and dogs
Across mountains and valleys
But here across the tablecloth
In our small flat
When she asks for the sugar
The teacups tremble
And a tidal wave foments
In the eddies of the cherry trifle.

Star Gazing

At midnight through my window
I spy with wondering eye
The far-off stars and planets
Sprinkled on the sky.

There the constant North Star
Hangs above our trees
And there the Plough and Sirius
And the distant Pleiades

Star on star past counting
Each one a raging sun
And the sky one endless suburb
With all her lights left on.

How strange it is that certain stars
Whose distant lights still glow
Vanished in that sea of space
Three million years ago.

And if I stare too long a time
The stars swim in my eyes
Drifting towards my bedroom
Down the vast slope of the skies.

And, mesmerized, I wonder,
Will *our* Earth someday die?
Spreading her fabric and her dreams
In fragments on the sky.

And then my imagination
Sees in some distant dawn
A young girl staring skywards
On a planet still unborn.

And will she also wonder,
Was there ever life out there?
Before the whole thing vanished
Like a dream into the air.

Launderette

Wishy, washy, there's my shirt
Swirling squirming round my vest.
Splashy, dashy, two red socks
In a sandwich with the rest.
A football scarf, a bright-red hat
A pillow-slip, blue jeans, a sheet.
Oh, my goodness, what was that?
A hand, a face, a pair of feet
Someone swirling round quite bare –
How did Granny get in there?

The Secret

Down a secret path
Through a secret wood
By the shore of a secret sea
I creep on tiptoe
To a place that I know
That no one has seen except me
Except me
That no one has seen except me.

And the soft wind that blows
Through the briar and the rose
That I pass along the way
Seems to whisper low,
Nobody must know
The secret you've learned today
Today
The secret you've learned today.

Down by a beach
Where the herring gulls screech
And the long white breakers roll
The voice of the sea
Whispers softly to me,
You must not tell a soul
A soul
You must not tell a soul.

But my secret somehow
Seems to grow and grow
Till it weighs me down like a load
Oh, I must tell someone
Before very long
Or I think I'm going to explode
Explode
Or I think I'm going to explode.

I climb from the beach
Till I finally reach
A valley, deep and wide
And it's there that I tell
To an old stone well
The secret I carry inside
Inside
The secret I carry inside.

In that well's stone ear
Where no one can hear
I whisper secretly
And from far away
Each word I say
Comes echoing back to me
To me
Comes echoing back to me.

And I make that well
Promise never to tell
What I've whispered so secretly
Then clear as a bell
Speaks the voice of the well,
'Your secret is safe with me
With me
Your secret is safe with me.'

School Outing

Class Four, isn't this wonderful?
Gaze from your windows, do.
Aren't those beauteous mountains heavenly?
Jut drink in that gorgeous view.

Sir, Linda Frost has fainted
Aw Sir, I think she's dead
And Kenny Mound's throwing sandwiches round
I've got ketchup all over my head.

Oh, aren't these costumes just super?
Please notice the duchess's hat!
You can write up your notes for homework tonight,
I know you'll look forward to that.

Sir, Antoinette Toast says she's seen the ghost
Of that woman, Lady Jane Grey
And I don't know where Billy Beefcake is
But the armour is walking away.

And here in this ghastly dungeon
The prisoners were left to die
Oh, it's all just so terribly touching
I'm afraid I'm going to cry.

Sir, Stanley Slack has put Fred on the rack
Sir, somebody's pinched my coat
Sir, Melanie Moreland's dived off the wall and
Is doing the crawl round the moat.

Well, here we are, homeward bound again –
It's been a wonderful day
I know when you meet your parents and friends
You'll have so many things to say.

Sir, what is that siren wailing for?
Sir, what's that road block ahead?
Sir, Tommy Treat is under the seat
Wearing a crown on his head.

Postbox

When Poppy posted
Pappy's post
She slyly peered within
And what a shock
Poor Poppy got
When a long hand
Pulled her in!

Rosie McAluskey

From a standing start
The two of us
Can race the leccy train
Out of Ainsdale Station
To the first telegraph pole
Where the sandhills begin.
The live line crackles
And smells of lightning.
'One foot on that
And you're nowt
But a pile of smoking ash,'
Rosie tells me smiling.
'Mr Rimmer's dog ran on it
Last Christmas Eve
And there was nowt to bury.'

She's full of tales like these:
The woman who swallowed a python's egg;
The whale that was thrown up on the beach
With a Ford van in its stomach
And the driver still alive;
The man who cleaned the chimney
And his wife came back
And lit a fire.

We watch a sparrow settle
On the length of steel.
He hops and sings to us
While the murderous voltage
Pours beneath his feet.
My dad has told me
All there is to know
Of electricity and death.
Sparrows are safe
As long as they're not earthed.
'Unless,' says Rosie,
'They have one leg
That's really long.'

We walk down Station Road,
Our four eyes skinned
For limping sparrows
With uneven legs.
It's for things like this,
I try to tell the gang,
I walk home
With Rosie McAluskey.

The Hedgehog

Look, here he comes a-visiting
My bristle brush, my mate
Up from the bottom privet hedge
To my breakfast plate.
Here he comes a-trundling
On his jacked-up legs
Past our Megan's washing
And the string bag full of pegs.
Eh, I'm glad to see thee, Mister
Good morning, how d'you do?
With your hunched back full of arrows
And your black nose wet with dew.
Don't need no invitation
To pleasure my old eye
Come up and see me any time
My hedgerow Samurai.

A Young Girl Came Riding

A young girl came riding
Through the mists of dawn
Where the moon's pale light
Cast a stream of white
Through the standing corn.

Her eyes they shone like amethyst
Her brow was ivory
Her yellow hair
In the dawn's sweet air
Streamed like the starlit sea.

Silent as dew to the meadow
Silent as light to the day
Silent as breath
In the mouth of death
She came where the sick girl lay.

She sang an ancient carol
Born in reverie
While her mare in the sedge
At the woodland edge
Cropped the grasses soundlessly.

A young girl came riding
Through the fields of May
But the sun's bright eye
In the morning sky
Saw two girls ride away.

Badger

I caught last night in the headlight's beam
My neighbour Brock again
Rolling his raggedy backside
Ambling along the lane
Like some old and weary farmhand
Strolling homeward from the inn;
Never hurried in his life
Too old now to begin.
I imagined him crossing his threshold
Turning the key in the lock
Settling down by the fireside
And grumbling to Mrs Brock:
'Who you reckon I seed just now
Roaring around the place?
Only that crack-brained wazzuck
One of they human race
A-driving his flash girt motor
Round the place again
Lights a-blazing, honking his horn
You'd think he owned our lane.'

Before the Beginning

Sometimes in dreams I imagine
Alone and unafraid
I'm standing in the darkness
When the first bright stars were made.

When the sun sprang out of the blackness
And lit the world's first dawn
When torrents of rock rained upwards
And the mountains and seas were born.

And I'm there when the forests and meadows
Flowered for the very first time
When eyeless legless creatures
Oozed upwards out of the slime.

But when I awake and read the books
Though they tell me more and more
The one thing they never tell me is –
What was there before . . .

Rubble

Pam found them;
Five small kittens
Huddled, fumbling, blind and wet
Beside the broken generator
In the crumbling outhouse
Pete and Frank were pulling down.
The mother didn't have a name.
'Must have wandered in
From one of the farms above the hill,'
My mother said
Tickling the tabby behind the ears.
'What d'you think this is, puss?
A maternity hospital?'

One by one we found
New homes for four of them.
Even the tabby mother
Didn't come to her saucer one day
And that was the last we saw of her.
The boisterous ginger
We adopted by default
Since no one seemed to want him;
Something in the glinting of his eye
Made prospective owners
Mumble some excuse
And walk away.
Rubble, we christened him
In honour of the place
Where he was born
And he was trouble from the start.

Pavarotti of the night
From early days
He fell in love with stars
And sang them endless, raucous arias
That would have jerked
The graveyard dead
To channering wakefulness.
Then with the dawn
He'd totter home
Weary, punch-drunk, scarred,
And flop upon the couch
Before the fire
Like some old bruiser
Waiting for the water
And the flapping towel.
Most days, by way of thanks
He'd drop a tiny corpse;
A mouse, a squirrel or a mole
Upon our slate doorstep
Then lick his folded paw
And preen himself,
Lazily surveying his fiefdom
Like a battered warlord
Fresh returned from victory in the field.
Then later on as he grew older
He'd crawl upon your lap
Blink slow his yellow eyes
Purr like a dynamo in bliss
And let you with some grace
Scratch him beneath the chin
Just long enough to let you think,
– At last, the old warrior's
Settling down and growing soft

Before, when least expected,
He'd unsheath his needling claws
And sink them deep as agony
Into the softness of your flesh.
All this while flashing you
The beatific smile that said,
'You can't imagine
The pleasure I derive
From simply being
What I am.'

Basil

When Cousin Basil
Played his bassoon
His body blew up
Like a barrage balloon
When I asked him shouldn't
He suck not blow
He swiftly answered
NOOOOOOOOOOOOOOOOOOOOOOOOOOOOOOOOOOO
OOOOOOOOOOOOOOOOOOOOOOOOOOOOOOOOOOO
OOOOOOOOOOOOOOOOOOOOOOOOOOOOOOOOOOO
OOOOOOOOOOOOOOOOOOOOOOOOOOOOOOOOOOO
OOOOOOOOOOOOOOOOOOOOOOO
OOOOOOOOOOOOOOO
OOOOOOO
OOOO
OO
O
   O
      O
         O
            O
               O
                  O
                     O
                        O
                           O
                              O
                                 O

Bedmobile

I hear my grandad on the stair
He's counting, One Two Three
Bringing a rosy apple plucked
From my special climbing tree.
He brings the garden in with him
The flowers and the air
And there are twigs and petals
Tangled in his hair.
And as I eat my apple
He sits down next to me
Turning an imaginary wheel
'Where to today?' says he.
And we drive our deluxe Bedmobile
To school along the heath
With the apple dribbling sweetness
Clenched between my teeth.

A Poem for a Very Special Person

Listen
Will you do something for me?
Will you?
I want you to read this poem
Silently, carefully
And don't look surprised
When you find out
Who it's about.
Are you ready with your
'I'm not surprised' look?
Wait for it
This poem is about . . .
    YOU!
          YES YOU!
Well then, how does it feel
To have a poem written about you?
What d'you mean you don't like it?
Staring?
Of course they're all staring,
That's the whole point.
What's that?
You wish the poem had been about someone else?
I would have to pick on you, wouldn't I?
Look why not point back?

Make out it's one of them.
Go on. Point at somebody.
No, not him
Nobody would write a poem about him.

Or her
Or . . .
Well, maybe.
It's not working?
They're still staring?
You're not enjoying this too much, are you?
You see
That's another thing I know about you
You're one of those people
Who doesn't like
Having poems written about them.
Hurt? Me, hurt?
Of course I'm not hurt.
Poets are used to that sort of thing.
Tell you what. Here's a thought.
Just quietly, secretly
Close the book and
Slip it into your desk.
Wait!
Better still
Just leave it lying about
In a public place.

Someone is bound to pick it up
And think the poem is about them.
People are like that.

Pearl

Pearl Jemima
Alfreton-Hughes
Turned into a light bulb
And blew her fuse
Out in the town
They noticed her plight
By the switch on her back
And her head burning bright
When she fell asleep
This light-hearted girl
Hung upside down
Like a fifty watt Pearl
'*Please*,' begged Pearl
With a nervous cough,
'*Whatever you do
Don't switch me off.*'

Eat It All Up

Skinny Denise looked at her tea
And wouldn't touch a thing
Said her mother, 'My dear, you're not going out
Till you've eaten up everything.'

'Everything, Mother?' said Skinny Denise
Shuffling in her seat
Then she picked up her knife and fork and began
To eat and eat and eat.

She drenched the cod in strawberry jam
While her mother watched in a daze
As her daughter washed three kippers down
With a gallon of mayonnaise.

'Manners, my dear!' her mother said,
But nothing could stop Denise
As she tore into fifteen Eccles cakes
Spaghetti and mushy peas.

Now all the food had disappeared
But she hadn't finished yet
She began to chew the tablecloth
The mat and the serviette.

Then she attacked the table
Without using knife or fork
Crunching the legs between her teeth
As if they were steaks of pork.

When the TV set went the way of the rest
Her parents stared in dismay
As a voice within Denise announced,
'Here is the News for Today.'

Next to go was the Afghan rug
The windows, the fireplace, the doors
The sofa, the chairs – they all disappeared
Into those cavernous jaws.

The floorboards made her lick her lips
The taste of the walls made her sigh
And when she'd eaten the ceiling and roof
For afters she ate the sky.

Her mother sat in the ruins and asked,
'What was all that about?'
'I ate it all up,' said Skinny Denise,
'So now may I please go out?'

There and Back Again

Benny went ballooning
Across the countryside
Beyond the cliffs of Dover
Across the oceans wide.
He took with him his lurcher dog
And some mincemeat for his tea
And a change of clothes for Sunday best
And a Chinese dictionary.
The sun shone down on Benny
It shone down on the Earth
It glistened on the dolphins
Who leapt and smiled with mirth.
And Benny saw a million sights
No man had seen before
So he flew across to Africa
And saw ten million more.
Then as he flew back home, he thought,
How famous I will be.
But his mother shouted, 'Wash your hands
Before you have your tea.'

Turkey and Pig

Said the Turkey to the Pig
With his feathers all awry,
'We must dance a flaunty jig
Before we have to fly.
With my clogs upon my feet
Let us dance into the blue.'
And the Pig he snorted, '*Oink oink*'
And the Turkey said, '*Gobble gobble goo.*'

Said the Pig unto the Turkey,
'Oh, tell me, where are you?
The weather's turned quite murky
And the fog's like Irish Stew.
The débutantes are smirking
The orchestra's on cue.'
And the Pig snorted, '*Oink oink*'
And the Turkey said, '*Gobble gobble goo.*'

Said the Turkey to the Pig,
'Have you noticed my new dress?
I ran it up this morning
Out of dill and watercress
I shall flirt with yon euphonium
Tell me his name dear, do.'
Said the Pig, '*I think it's Oink Oink
Or possibly Gobble Gobble Goo.*'

'My joy is semolina,'
Ran Pig's jocular refrain.
'One can get it from the Queena
One can get it on the brain.
If the orchestra would play it
To an air I heard in Crewe
I'll do the honours on the *oink oink*
If you'll sing *gobble gobble goo*.'

Quoth the Turkey quite infuriate,
'You are stepping on my clothes
And there's a dwarfish curiate
Who is peering up my nose.
Oh, Piglet, I'm convulsed with shame
Whatever shall I do?'
And the Pig said, '*You try oink oink
And I'll try gobble gobble goo*.'

'We're caviar to the general
And leek soup to the rest
We have raced with fourteen tandems
And shown them who is best.
We have marched on whelks through Asia
And loved in Kathmandoooooooooooo
Oh, the world has heard our *oink oink*
And our *gobble gobble gobble gobble goo*.'

So that is where we leave them
On the uncharted shores of Time
Knowing naught can ever grieve them
While they're running through this rhyme
For they're dancing down a road of dreams
Hand in hand into the blue
And the shadows echo back their song,
Oink oink and *gobble gobble goo*.

Scatterbrain

Before he goes to bed at night
Scatterbrained Uncle Pat
Gives the clock a saucer of milk
And winds up the tabby cat.

Index of First Lines